P9-CSE-654

Woolly Thoughts

Unlock Your Creative Genius with Modular Knitting

Pat Ashforth and
Steve Plummer

Dover Publications, Inc.
Mineola, New York

Copyright

Copyright © 1994 by Pat Ashforth and Steve Plummer
All rights reserved.

Bibliographical Note

This Dover edition, first published in 2007, is an unabridged republication of
the work originally published as *Woolly Thoughts: How to Unlock Your Creative
Genius* by Souvenir Press, London, in 1994.

Library of Congress Cataloging-in-Publication Data

Ashforth, Pat.
    Woolly thoughts : unlock your creative genius with modular knitting / Pat
Ashforth and Steve Plummer.
        p. cm.
    Reprint. Originally published: London : Souvenir Press, under title: Woolly
thoughts : how to unlock your creative genius, 1994.
    ISBN-13: 978-0-486-46084-0
    ISBN-10: 0-486-46084-3
    1. Knitting. I. Plummer, Steve. II. Title.

TT820.A8788 2007
746.43'2041—dc22

                                                                            2007012778

Manufactured in the United States of America
Dover Publications, Inc., 31 East 2nd Street, Mineola, N.Y. 11501

Contents

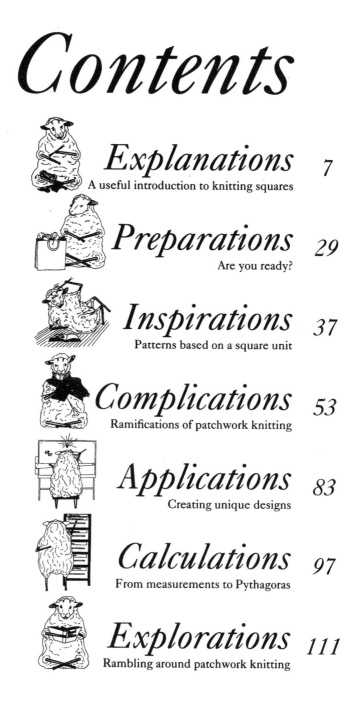

METRIC EQUIVALENCY CHART
CENTIMETRES TO INCHES
[CONVERSION FORMULA: centimetres x 0.394 = inches]

0.3 cm	0.6	1.3	1.6	1.9	2.2	2.5	3.2	3.8	4.4
⅛ in	¼	½	⅝	¾	⅞	1	1¼	1½	1¾

5.1	6.4	7.6	8.9	10.2	11.4	12.7	15.2	17.8	20.3
2	2½	3	3½	4	4½	5	6	7	8

22.9	25.4	30.5	33	35.6	38.1	40.6	43.2	45.7	48.3
9	10	12	13	14	15	16	17	18	19

50.8	53.3	55.9	58.4	61.0	63.5	66.0	68.6	71.1	73.7
20	21	22	23	24	25	26	27	28	29

WEIGHT CONVERSION CHART
GRAMS TO OUNCES
[CONVERSION FORMULA: grams x 0.035 = ounces]

28 gr	57	85	113	142	170	198	227
1 oz	2	3	4	5	6	7	8

255	283	312	340	369	397	425	454
9	10	11	12	13	14	15	16

KNITTING NEEDLE CONVERSION CHART
METRIC SIZES
U.S. SIZES
CANADIAN & U.K SIZES

2.0	2.25	2.75	3.0	3.25	3.5	3.75	4.0	4.5	5.0	5.5
0	1	2	-	3	4	5	6	7	8	9
14	13	12	11	10	-	9	8	7	6	5

6.0	6.5	7.0	7.5	8.0	9.0	10.0	12.0	16.0	19.0	25.0
10	10½	-	-	11	13	15	17	19	35	50
4	3	2	1	0	00	000	-	-	-	-

Explanations

FORGET
ALL THE
RULES

Forget about following conventional instructions and charts

Forget about being unable to mix different yarns

Forget about blocking and pressing pieces

Forget about complicated stitches

Forget about buying patterns

Forget about tension

Create and knit your own
designs using simple stitches
and shapes in the colours
and textures of your choice.
Get exactly what you want by
putting together squares and other
simple shapes to make larger squares
and rectangles, although the basic
shapes might be difficult to spot in the
finished product.

Once you understand the basic ideas,
which rely on mathematical accuracy
and knowing how to cheat when
things go wrong, the possibilities
are endless.

Use these methods to make any
garment you choose. You can also create wall-hangings,
rugs, bags, blankets, and many other items.

Don't be restricted by what books and patterns tell you
to do. Do what you want to do. Use your own ideas.

All you need
is yarn, needles,
a tape measure,
a calculator and
imagination

WHY SHOULD I WORK IN SQUARES?

It's more interesting than following conventional instructions.

Working in small pieces has advantages for beginners and for experienced knitters.

Your garment will be the right size. You will never again knit something that is too long, too short, too big or too tight.

You are always working with small pieces, so they are quick to make and any mistakes can be quickly spotted and put right.

Patchwork knitting is quicker and more flexible than fabric patchwork. It can be made into warm clothes or decorative items.

You can use many different shades and yarns but only ever work with one at a time. This makes it quicker and easier. The yarns cannot get tangled.

Squares, and other shapes, can be put together in much the same way as patchwork fabric. It can cover any area or shape you choose.

You can use yarns of different thicknesses in the same garment without problems.

Two or more people can knit parts of the same garment. The pieces will fit together because you are always working with measurements, not numbers of stitches.

HOW TO KNIT A SQUARE

Learning how to knit an accurate square is the most important part of this book. There are several ways of knitting a 'square'. The method shown here is one of the few that is suitable and accurate enough for geometric designs.

If you already know how to knit, follow the written instructions opposite. If you are not yet a knitter, follow the step-by-step pictures on pages 14-17. You might want to ask an experienced knitter for advice but *you must make your square in this way*.

Work in garter stitch all the time.

Row 1 – Make a slip knot and knit into it twice
          (once in the front, once in the back).

Row 2 – Knit the first stitch and knit twice into the
          second stitch.

Row 3 – Knit the first two stitches and knit twice into
          the last stitch.

Row 4 – Knit until you reach the last stitch, then knit
          twice into the last stitch.

You should now have a small triangle.

Repeat row 4.

Every two rows adds one ridge to the triangle.

Repeat row 4 until the sides of the square are the length
you want.

When the square is the correct width, complete it by
knitting together the last two stitches in every row until
two stitches remain.

    Knit the last two stitches together and fasten off
by cutting the yarn about 15 cm from the knitting and
pulling the end through the last stitch.

    You should have the same number of ridges in the
second half of the square as you had in the first half.

1 Make a loop in the yarn and put it on the left needle.

2 Tighten the loop a little. Put the right needle through the loop, going behind the left needle.

3 Wind the yarn round the right needle, from the back.

4 Pull this loop through with the right-hand needle. Do not let the other loop fall off.

5 Put the right needle through the back of the left loop. Wind the yarn round the right needle, from the back.

6 Pull this loop through with the right-hand needle. Pull the left needle out now.

7 You have two stitches on the right needle. Turn the needle round so it becomes the left needle ready for the next row.

8 Put the new right-hand needle through the front of the first loop on the left needle, going behind that needle.

9 Wind the yarn round the right needle from the back.

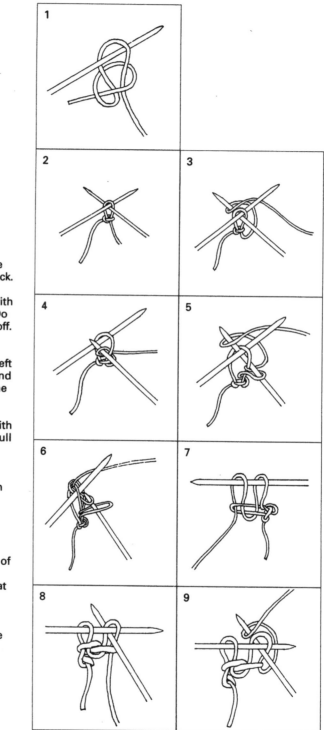

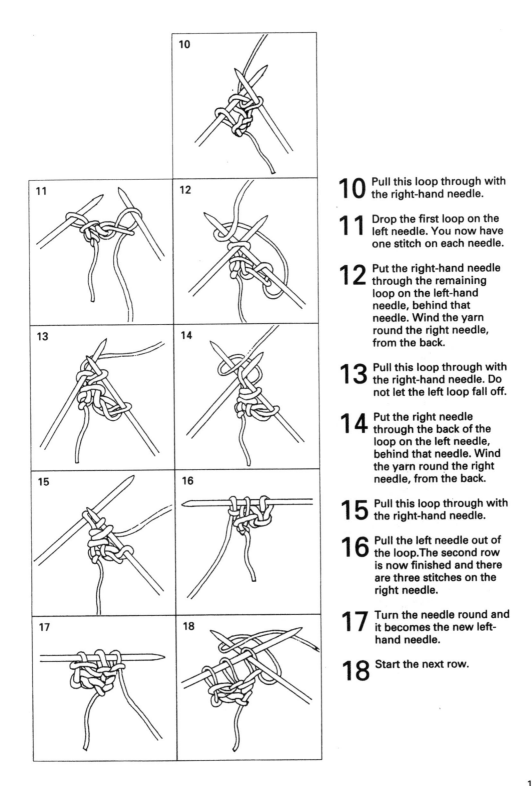

10 Pull this loop through with the right-hand needle.

11 Drop the first loop on the left needle. You now have one stitch on each needle.

12 Put the right-hand needle through the remaining loop on the left-hand needle, behind that needle. Wind the yarn round the right needle, from the back.

13 Pull this loop through with the right-hand needle. Do not let the left loop fall off.

14 Put the right needle through the back of the loop on the left needle, behind that needle. Wind the yarn round the right needle, from the back.

15 Pull this loop through with the right-hand needle.

16 Pull the left needle out of the loop. The second row is now finished and there are three stitches on the right needle.

17 Turn the needle round and it becomes the new left-hand needle.

18 Start the next row.

Continue in the same way. Knit each stitch except the last one in each row, following steps 8, 9, 10 and 11. When you reach the last stitch of each row make an extra stitch by following steps 12, 13, 14, 15 and 16. Each row will be one stitch longer than the one before and your shape will be a triangle. Carry on until the triangle you have is half the square you need.

You have been knitting garter stitch, increasing one stitch at the end of each row. To complete the square, continue in garter stitch and knit together the last two stitches in each row so that each row has one stitch fewer than the row before.

You are now knitting garter stitch and decreasing one stitch at the end of each row. Continue until you have two stitches left. Knit those two together, cut the yarn, leaving about 15 cm, and fasten off by putting the end of the yarn through the final stitch and pulling tight.

TO KNIT TWO TOGETHER :

Put the right needle through the front of both stitches, at the same time, and knit like a normal stitch.

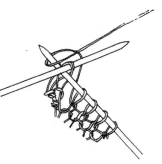

WHAT IS GARTER STITCH? WHY SHOULD I BOTHER WITH IT?

Everything in this book is made entirely in garter stitch.

Garter stitch means every row is made up only of knit stitches. In some books these are called plain stitches or plain knitting. You do not need to learn how to do purl stitches.

It is often thought of as a beginner's stitch and is rarely used once other stitches have been learned. This is a shame because it is very versatile if it is used to make a soft fabric. Some patterns use it for edgings because it can be made very firm, but it doesn't have to be like that. It will never make a smooth surface and it makes a slightly thicker fabric than the same yarn would do if it were used for some other stitches, but it can be just as comfortable if the fabric you create is soft.

If you have followed the instructions for making a square you have been working in garter stitch with an increase or decrease at the end of every row. Normal garter stitch knits into each stitch only once and has sides perpendicular to the rows.

There are several advantages of garter stitch.

1. You only need to learn one stitch.

2. It is easy.

3. The knitting always stays flat so does not need any edging to finish it off if you keep it neat while you are working.

4. Measuring is easy and accurate because the work does not curl up at the edges and have to be straightened out.

5. Counting rows is very easy. One ridge is two rows.

6. It forms perfect squares, and other shapes, in a way that no other knitting can.

7. Pieces can be joined edge-to-edge so that they lie flat and the joins make no difference to the size.

8. You can change the appearance by turning pieces round with the ridges going in different directions.

9. It looks the same on both sides, if you are working in one colour. Where you change colour the front and back look different.

WHY DO I HAVE TO KNIT THE SQUARES DIAGONALLY?

If you have ever knitted a square before you probably had instructions that told you how many stitches to cast on and how many rows to knit. Working in garter stitch you would almost certainly have got a square but it might not have been the size you intended. Some people knit tightly, some loosely. You would need to knit a square to find out how big a square you would make. That seems a waste of time to me.

Knitting diagonally the square will always be the right size first time. You can work with any yarn you like, any needles you happen to have (as long as they are a matching pair) and change yarn from one square to the next. The squares will all be exactly right. You will never need to do a test to see what size you will get. Tension squares are not needed with this method.

If you are still not convinced, go and find some friends and experiment. Each of you knit a square, in the same yarn, with 20 stitches and 40 rows of garter stitch. You will find two problems. Firstly, the squares will not be the same size. Secondly some of you will have untidy tops and bottoms to your square, and some may have become so curved at the top they aren't squares at all.

Now decide what size square you want to make, cut it out of a piece of paper or card and knit again using the diagonal method. Keep increasing at the ends of the rows until your shape fits the card, then start decreasing. Compare the squares when you have finished. They will be almost identical in size, although some will have more tightly packed rows and stitches than others.

BASIC JUMPER SHAPE

Now you know how to make squares you can make a simple jumper without knowing anything else. Make lots of small squares, or a few large ones, and stitch them together. (See page 35 for advice on stitching.)

For your first attempt at your own design it is best to start with these simple shapes.

You only need to know the width and length of your garment before you can begin knitting. Then you can decide how to create your first large rectangle for the back. The other pieces will evolve from this.

This is the basic shape of a jumper.

If you could open it up it would look like this.

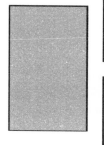

If you took it to pieces it would look like this.

The best way to decide how big to make your new jumper is to measure an old one of the right size. You will probably be surprised how much bigger than you your clothes are.

To measure the rectangle for the back, put the garment you are going to measure flat on the floor or table. If it has buttons, fasten it up first. Smooth it out but do not stretch it. Measure the length of the back from the top of the shoulder. Measure the width of the garment at the widest part, which is usually just below where the sleeves are joined on.

If the garment is pulled in by a band at the bottom it may not look like a rectangle, so try to imagine the shape before the band was added. Decide whether to measure the whole length or only to the top of the band, leaving room to add a band later.

If you want your new garment to be fitted at the bottom it will have to have a band of some sort, otherwise it will be completely straight. A band can be shaped or straight, any depth you want, and can be used to alter the finished length of the garment. (You can read more about alterations later.)

If you want to plan farther ahead you can take other measurements from your old garment now. You will need to know the dimensions of the sleeves. and neck.

Necklines vary a great deal in shape. Ignore any neckband or collar and measure the width and depth of the opening.

Sleeves often have tighter bands at the wrist. Try to measure the size the sleeves would be if they were not being pulled in by the bands.

The length of a sleeve should be measured from the point where the underneath of the sleeve joins the body. Measure at right angles to the top and bottom of the sleeve, not along the sloping seam. Remember to allow for a band at the wrist if you want one.

The width at the top of the sleeve should be measured where the sleeve joins the back.

Measure the width at the bottom of the sleeve while someone else is stretching the band for you.

WHAT SIZE SQUARES SHOULD I KNIT?

When you know the length and width of the large rectangle for the back you can decide how to divide it into squares. A calculator might be useful although the maths is very simple.

You need to find a number that will divide into both of the measurements to give you squares of a size that you would be able to work with. A square of about 10 cm is probably a good size to start with but the choice is entirely yours.

Small squares mean lots of sewing up afterwards but they also give you much more flexibility in the arrangement of colours.

Large squares need less sewing but limit the number of positions where they can be placed.

Some people get bored making lots of small pieces, others think it seems to take longer if they have to make big pieces.

Small pieces are very convenient if you carry your knitting around with you.

If necessary adapt the rectangle to make other sizes of squares fit into it.

You probably won't notice if you have to change the width of your garment by a few centimetres.

The rectangles for the sleeves will be smaller than the back but you will almost certainly be able to make them from the same size squares if you are prepared to make small alterations to the width of the sleeve tops.

You do not have to use the same size squares for the sleeves as for the front and back. You could choose squares to suit the amount of yarn you have. Make squares from as many different types and shades of yarn as you like.

The rectangle for the front is the same as the one for the back and will need the same number of squares.

When you know the sizes for your squares, draw them on paper and check every square you knit against the drawings.

Do whatever you want to do. Just be sure that you know what size you will get when you put the squares together.

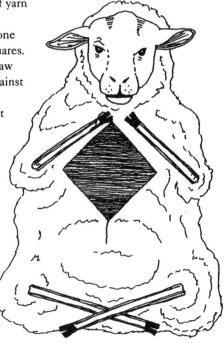

TELL ME
AGAIN,
SIMPLY.
WHAT DO
I DO?

Triangles.   Squares.

Find your yarn and needles.

Take measurements to make four rectangles - back, front, two sleeves.

Decide how many squares will cover the rectangles and work out how big they have to be.

Draw squares of all the sizes you need.

Knit your squares, measuring them against your drawings.

Join the squares to make a jumper.

NEXT

Now you know the basic ideas involved you will be ready to start making your first garment. If you have ever knitted anything before you probably do not need any more advice; if you are a complete beginner you might need to know a bit about the yarn and needles to choose and how to join your garment together. You will find that information in **Preparations.**

Once you have mastered these ideas you should be ready to go on adapting them to provide an infinite variety of shapes, sizes, colours and designs. **Inspirations** should give you ideas, if you need more.

Complications has lots of practical information which you might need to be able to fulfil the ideas in your imagination. It will tell you about adjustments that can be made to the basic jumper shape, and other items that can be made. It gives other ways of joining the pieces of your patchwork and lots of information about finishing your work. There is more about the yarns you might want to use and how to "create" your own yarns. The final part of this section might help you get out of a mess when things start to go wrong.

Some of the designs I have created are shown in **Applications**, together with an outline of how they were made. There are no patterns, only ideas from my own experiments and experience.

In **Calculations** you will find some of the mathematics that could be helpful in creating your own designs. (It isn't difficult.)

Explorations is....find out for yourself, by exploration.

This book will not tell you all you ever wanted to know about knitting. It is limited to the techniques you are likely to need to complete garments using nothing but garter stitch patchwork. Use it as a source of ideas, not a manual of how things should be done.

Use your **IMAGINATION.**

Preparations

PREPARE TO START

The yarns you are most likely to use are:

4 ply
This is rather thin and needs patience to knit a lot of squares. It can be used double, or with another thinner yarn. Use two strands of the same colour or mix your own colours.

Double knitting
This is the thickness most commonly found. It is very popular and can usually be bought cheaply. It comes in a very wide range of colours and textures.

Aran
This is thicker than double knitting and comes in a narrower range of colours.

Chunky
This is thick and the work grows quickly but it can be expensive because each ball knits very few squares. A completed garment can be heavy to wear and difficult to wash.

As soon as you start looking for yarn you will find a confusingly large range. How can you know which to choose?

When you are designing your own garments there are no right or wrong yarns. The choice is entirely up to you but you will probably soon decide which you like working with. Different types of yarn create visibly different effects and the fibre content can affect the properties, like warmth and washability, of the finished garment. I can only give you a little information and a few suggestions about what to look at first. After that you will have to find out more by experimentation.

A smooth double knitting yarn might be easiest to begin with.

Do not take any notice of the conventional uses of yarns. If you like the look of something, try it and see what happens. If you fancy a jumper in pastel colours there is no reason why you should not use baby wool to knit it, even though you are unlikely to find manufacturers' patterns using baby wool for adults.

If your wool shop happens to have a stock of dishcloth cotton and you want a jumper in those shades of cream and beige, then give it a try. You won't look as though you are wearing the dishcloth and no one but you will ever know what you used.

Use whatever you want whenever you want, bearing in mind one or two minor exceptions. Clothes and toys for babies and small children should never be made of fluffy yarns or anything else with fibres that could come off and choke them.

Some people are allergic to certain fibres or do not like the feel of them, so if you are knitting for someone else, check first.

CHOOSING YARNS
You can use any yarn you like. All the yarn in one square should be approximately

the same thickness but it can vary from square to square. You can use as many different weights as you want but remember that a heavy square could distort a lighter one. It is best not to make the weights too contrasting unless you have a special reason to do so.

You can use yarns with different content, e.g. wool, acrylic, cotton, etc. They will look and feel different and some will be warmer to wear than others.

If you mix fibres you will need to wash the garment by hand unless you are sure that all your yarns have the same washing instructions.

There are many factors that need to be taken into account when you choose your yarns. Some are shiny, others are not, so they could look odd together. If they create the effect you're trying to achieve they could be the right choice.

Some yarns are a single colour, others have more colours. The extra colours may be added with flecks, or several strands being twisted together, or space-dyed yarns where you can see different colours along the length of the yarn.

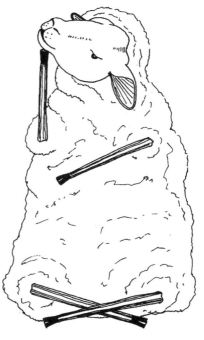

Textured yarns and fluffy yarns will blur the edges of the shapes you make. If you think it is important for your pieces to be well-defined your best choice might be a plain, smooth yarn.

There are many other, more unusual, yarns. Some of them are expensive. Look in the shops to see what is available and perhaps consider using some of them for small parts of your garment. If you want to know more, look in your library for a book that tells you about yarns in more detail.

The choice is endless and it's up to you to make the decision. Commercial patterns always tell you what to use and they often tell you what shade to use as well. Now you have to do all the thinking for yourself.

PREPARE TO KNIT

The size of needles to use will depend on the yarn you choose and how tight your knitting is. Forget anything you've read about tension. Aim for knitting that feels right. Try various sizes to find out what you like.

If your knitting feels too hard and stiff the work is too tight because your needles are too thin. Try thicker ones. If the knitting is soft and floppy and easily pulls out of shape then your work is too loose. Try thinner needles.

The bands round balls of yarn give a suggested size of needle to use. Read the band but make your own decision.

Try the following sizes for yourself. These are only suggestions and you may decide to use thicker or thinner. The sizes are metric with the old English sizes in brackets.

4 ply	3.00 (11)	3.25 (10)
D.K.	3.75 (9)	4.00 (8)
Aran	4.50 (7)	5.00 (6)
Chunky	6.00 (4)	6.50 (3)

NEEDLE SIZES Knitting needles are measured in millimetres throughout Europe, but if your needles are old they could be numbered according to the old English sizes. In the metric system higher numbers mean fatter needles. In the old system the opposite is true. It doesn't matter what your needles are called so long as they give you knitting that feels right to you and you can identify them if you should want to use them again.

They come in different lengths, the most common being 25, 30 and 35 cm. You will not usually need very long needles for knitting squares although you may need longer ones for some parts of your work.

It is possible to buy very short needles in a limited range of sizes. They are usually called children's knitting needles but they are very comfortable for anyone to work with when only small numbers of stitches are needed.

You can't use short needles if you have a lot of stitches. It is very frustrating to try to work with more stitches than will easily fit on the needle. Long needles can be used for any number of stitches and some people use them all the time but they can get in the way. Choose whatever length you feel most comfortable using

CIRCULAR NEEDLES You can also buy long 'circular needles'. These are like two short needles with a flexible plastic piece joining them. They come in all the same thicknesses as ordinary knitting needles and a variety of lengths.

You do not have to be knitting in a circle to use them. You can use the two ends of the needle like ordinary needles to knit backwards and forwards. If you decide to knit a band all the way round the bottom of your cardigan, in one go, you will need a circular needle as there will be too many stitches to fit on to ordinary needles. (For bands see **Complications** - Picking up stitches)

When you have a lot of stitches on the needle circular needles make the work easier to hold. If you have an enormous number of stitches you can even use two circular needles in the same way as you use ordinary needles.

Another good point about these needles is that when you leave work on them you can push the stitches to the middle and they are much less likely to fall off than they are from rigid needles. That can be useful if you want to make two pieces at the same time to be sure they are exactly alike. For instance, start both sleeves at the same time and work a section of one and then the same part on the other.

A circular needle is very versatile and doesn't cost much more than a pair of straight needles. You can use them all the time if you want to, for large or small pieces of work. If you have to buy new needles they could be worth considering.

CHOICE OF NEEDLES Needles come in a variety of materials. Again the choice must be a personal one.

Metal, or plastic-coated metal, needles are durable but can feel cold. Plastic is warmer to the touch but more likely to break. Many people who suffer from arthritis and rheumatism recommend bamboo needles. You might also come across wooden or bone needles.

Never attempt to work with bent or damaged needles because they will make your work uneven and try your patience.

If you have any problems with the needles you are using try some made from a different material. The needles that help you do the job most efficiently are the right ones for you.

Knitting in rounds If you decide to use your circular needle to knit round and round instead of backwards and forwards you will not get garter stitch. You will get a smoother fabric, called stocking stitch. The rules you learn in this book will not work.

Changing needles Once you have decided what size needles give the type of knitting you want you will probably always use the same size for each type of yarn. Bands up the front or round the bottom, neck or sleeves often need to be tighter or less flexible so should be knitted on thinner needles. (See **Complications** - Picking up stitches)

PREPARE TO SEW

1. Do not stitch too tightly. You could distort the shape.

2. Do not stitch too far over the edge. The join might not lie flat.

3. Fasten the beginning and end of the sewing securely. It could come undone.

4. Position all shapes carefully, matching corners, stripes, etc.

5. Keep checking. Open up the seam to make sure it lies flat and looks right.

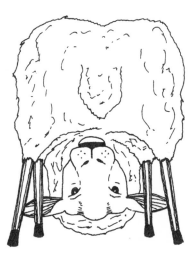

Poor making up can ruin a perfect piece of knitting. Put as much thought and effort into the assembly of the pieces as you did into knitting them.

Joining lots of small pieces can be tedious. Join as much as you can as you go along. This way you will not have a lot of making up to do at the end and you will be able to see if your design is coming out as you intended. You will be able to make alterations if you find something does not work or if you change your mind.

Unless your garment is made from identical squares you will have several different types of edges to join. You could be trying to match pieces that do not look the same. Whatever the edges are like there are a few important points to remember.

PREPARING FOR SEWING Stitching has to be done with care and accuracy if you want the shapes to stay the size you planned.

You will need a needle with a large eye for making up. You can buy needles especially for this job from your wool shop. As with any other equipment you need to buy, needles will last for a very long time if you look after them properly.

Sewing up should be done with the yarn you have been working with, if possible. There are times when you cannot use the same yarn because it is too thick to go through the needle, or too knobbly to stitch with, or, as occasionally happens, it falls apart when you stitch with it although it behaved perfectly well for knitting.

If you cannot use the same yarn find a similar one that is smoother and thinner. Do not be tempted to use thread for stitching up. It will pull your knitting out of shape and may even break if you make a sudden movement when you are wearing the garment.

PINS The only other equipment you will need for stitching up is pins. Any pins will do but long ones are best and those with coloured heads are less likely to get left in the knitting.

USING THE TAILS If there is a long tail of yarn hanging off your shape you could use that to begin the stitching. This will save you having to darn in so many ends afterwards.

All ends have to be darned in eventually. Never cut off a tail of yarn close to the knitting, your knitting might start to unravel. If you can't use an end for stitching up, weave it through a few stitches so that it is out of sight on the back, before cutting off.

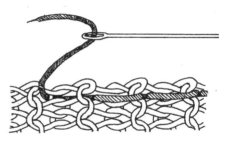

OVERSEWING
The pieces should be oversewn together as this enables them to lie side by side afterwards. Oversewing should not change the size of your pieces when you join them.

Put together the first two shapes with their right sides facing each other. Pin the pieces together to hold them in position while you stitch. You can take the pins out again, one at a time, as soon as they begin to get in the way of your stitching.

Use either a tail that is already attached or a new length of yarn, about 50 cm long. Secure the new yarn at the start of the join by stitching over the very edge of the join twice in the same place.

When the yarn is secure, work your way along the edge, stitching over and over, catching the edge of both pieces of knitting. Practice will tell you how far over the edge to stitch and how far apart the stitches should be. If it looks good on the right side it must be right.

BACKSTITCHING In a few places, where you have shaped pieces in a complicated way, it might be difficult to oversew seams and make them look tidy on the outside. If this happens you should join them with a backstitch seam as close to the edge as you can without causing any lumps and bumps to show on the outside.

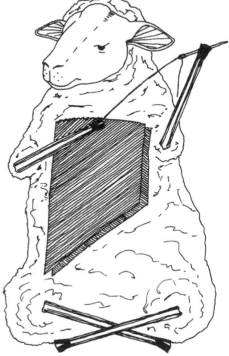

If you look closely at the edges you are joining you will notice that there are some knobbly bits and you will find that if you stitch through these your knitting is less likely to stretch than if you stitch through the other bits. You cannot always match up knobbles from both pieces so you might have to stitch through a knobble on one piece and not on the other.

At the end of the shapes, fasten off the yarn by stitching in the same place twice and threading the end back through your last few stitches, then cut off any remaining yarn. If you are going to join another shape in the same place, fasten off and continue using the same length of yarn for the next shape.

Inspirations

You have probably noticed that this is a knitting book almost totally devoid of colour. It is intended to make you think about shapes, how they fit together and how they can be used to cover any larger shape you choose. The colours you decide to use will be entirely up to you. If you want to know more about colour theory look in your library for a book, but use it only for ideas. There are no rules that can't be broken.

Because you will be working with fairly large blocks of colour, the colours are important. Every combination gives a different effect. Changing the place of one shape can change the effect of the entire garment. Once you have learned how to make the shapes and put them together you are free to examine the effects of colour whenever you want. You are much more likely to run out of time than ideas to experiment with.

Imagine the rectangle for the back of your jumper to be a canvas on which you are going to paint blocks of colour. In **Inspirations** the blocks will all be based on squares. In **Applications** they will be more ambitious shapes.

If you are trying to make a square for your back you can divide it into small squares in many different ways. All you need to do is to divide the width of the back by the number of squares you want going across it and you will have the length of the sides of the small squares.

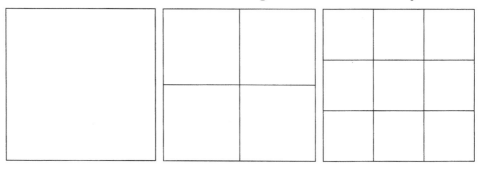

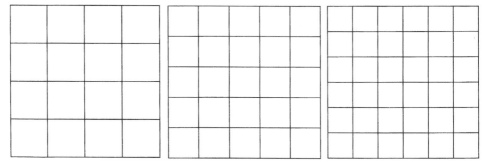

WIDTH OF BACK	NUMBER OF SQUARES ACROSS BACK OF GARMENT				
	2	3	4	5	6
30 cm	15	10	7.5	6	5
35cm	17.5	11.5	9	7	6
40 cm	20	13.5	10	8	6.5
45 cm	22.5	15	11	9	7.5
50 cm	25	16.5	12.5	10	8.5
55 cm	27.5	18.5	14	11	9
60 cm	30	20	15	12	10

The exact size of your squares will depend on the overall size you want to make the back of your garment. Use this table as a guide.

Measurements in the table are to the nearest half-centimetre

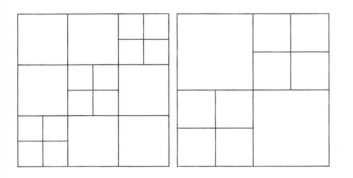

You can, of course, combine different sizes to make the overall size.

The back of your garment is more likely to be a rectangle than a square. You may have to alter the dimensions slightly to be able to fit squares into the shape. Before you decide to change either dimension you must decide whether the alterations would still produce a garment of the right size. Would it matter if your jumper was 2 cm wider than you planned? Would your jacket be long enough if it was 4 cm shorter? How much could you change each measurement by and still get what you want?

When you are sure you know what lengths and widths would be all right, go back to your original measurements and see what numbers will divide into both of them, or into numbers very close to them. There may be several sizes that would work out to give you a rectangle within the limits you have set yourself.

Here are a few examples which make rectangles close to 50 cm x 60 cm

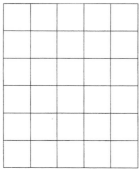

Width = 5 x 10 = 50 cm
Length = 6 x 10 = 60 cm

Width = 4 x 12 = 48 cm
Length = 5 x 12 = 60 cm

Width = 3 x 16 = 48 cm
Length = 4 x 16 = 64 cm

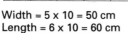

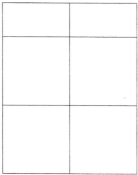

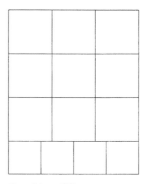

The half squares at the top of this rectangle are part of full squares which fit over the shoulders.
Width = 2 x 25 = 50 cm
Length = 2 x 25 + 12.5
        = 62.5 cm

Add a strip at the top of any squares to make up the length you want. It can accommodate all the neck shaping.
Width = 2 x 25 = 50 cm
Length = 2 x 25 + 10
        = 60 cm

Combine different squares to give the sizes you want.
Width = 3 x 16 = 48 cm
       (or 4 x 12 = 48 cm)
Length = 3 x 16 + 12
        = 60 cm

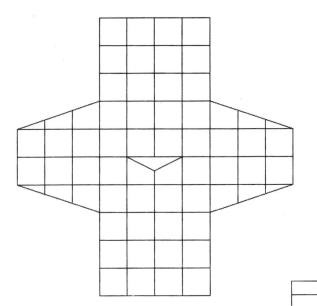

Now decide how the squares are going to cover the other pieces of your garment.

Garments vary according to the shape and preferences of the wearer. You may want yours to be similar to one of the diagrams shown here or you may need to draw your own diagram.

If you intend to add bands or cuffs afterwards, remember to make your garment, and sleeves, shorter than the finished length you need.

At the edges of the sleeves and on the neck there are some incomplete squares. If you want to avoid most of this shaping stick to the rectangular shapes used in **Explanations.** If you want to shape the sleeves read the sections on alterations in **Complications.**

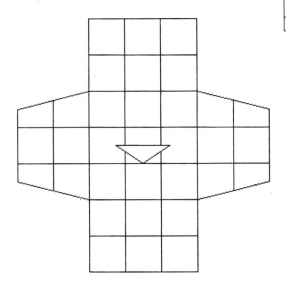

Check that your design will match at the side seams when you join the front to the back.

Use plain squares or try some of the designs on the next few pages. These are all based on simple two-colour squares in interesting patterns. They are shown on a 4 x 4 grid but could be adapted for other rectangles.

Knit the basic square in one colour up to the widest point and another colour for the other half.

All the patterns on pages 42 – 45 can be made from 16 identical squares.

Many other patterns can be made. Use squared paper to design your own.

Adapt the patterns to use with a different number of squares or to cover a rectangle instead of a square.

You could make the squares first and decide later how to assemble them.

You can create many designs with just two colours. These examples show the changes that can be made by reversing the colours. Different parts of the design become dominant. Choose your own colours to create the effect you would like. The shading can be very subtle or as contrasting as you want.

Adding extra colours leads to even more patterns, still using half-and-half squares.

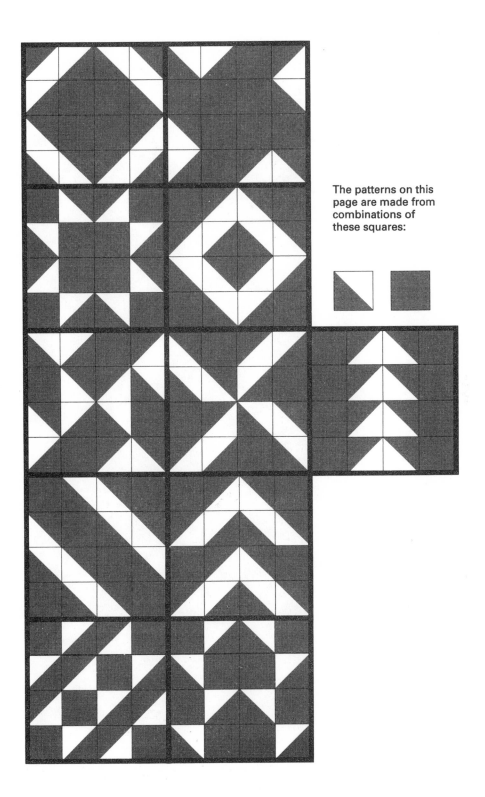

The patterns on this page are made from combinations of these squares:

These are some of the patterns that can be made from 16 of these:

These are some of the
patterns that can be
made from 16 of these:

COLOUR
INSPIRATIONS

All the patterns on the preceding pages can be made from simple squares. They can use just two colours or as many as you want.

.Build up a collection of colour ideas from pictures that interest you. It doesn't matter if your ideas originate from a flower, a racing car, a countryside scene or anything else. Try to see the combinations of colours, not the shapes. You might be surprised at the shades you like to see together.

I choose colours for a variety of reasons and sometimes for a combination of reasons. The new garment might need to tone with something else. I might accidentally find an interesting combination in my stockpile of yarn. Sometimes I want to use yarns again in a different design just to see what effect the changes make.

One jacket I knitted was in many shades of grey, from almost white to charcoal. It was the result of watching an old black and white film. Another was in equal amounts of mixed light greys and light yellows and was inspired by a postcard of the inside of a cave, where yellow light streaked the grey stone. A third was the result of watching the opening ceremony of the 1988 Seoul Olympics. The Dragon Drum, which was carried along the river, was painted in very deep shades of red, blue and green. I had not previously thought of using those colours together without something to brighten them up. The resulting cardigan was in many shades of rich jewel colours which would have lost their effect alongside anything brighter.

Take notice of what you see around you all the time.

If you keep your eyes open you will find interesting shapes and patterns everywhere. Many of them can be translated into knitting with only minor adaptations.

If you see a pattern you want to remember, make a record of it. You could make a sketch or perhaps take a photograph.

Ignore colours and look at shapes. You might not be able to use all of a design but you might extract some elements from it.

If you want to go looking for patterns, start in the library with books about patchwork. Many of the shapes used in fabric patchwork are basically the same as those described in **Complications.** You should also find ideas in the art or craft sections of the library. Ignore the techniques being described. Pick out ideas you can use.

Many of my ideas come from mathematics books and magazines. That is probably because I read them often. You are equally likely to find ideas in books you read.

I have used several ideas that have come from books about mosaics, which often have repeating geometric designs. Modern tiled floors can also provide inspiration. These may be in unexpected places, such as public toilets or motorway service stations.

On a holiday in Malta I noticed that almost all the church floors were geometric designs using the same three colours – black, white and yellow. While everyone else was admiring the magnificent buildings I was photographing floors.

Anything that is made largely from straight lines could generate a pattern. All forms of architecture are possibilities. Some of the patterns on the preceding pages can be found in medieval half-timbered buildings, others in ultra-modern office blocks. Look around you and notice what is there.

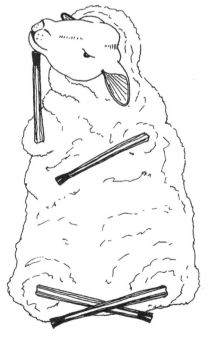

Complications

YARN

We still tend to talk about wool shops, not yarn shops, and yet much of the yarn you will find will be man-made, not from a sheep. Some will be pure wool, some will be completely man-made, some mixtures. Everyone understands what we mean when we talk about a ball of wool but to be technically correct we should usually be talking about yarn.

NON-YARNS You can knit with any yarn you like and also with some materials that do not fit into the category of yarns. Anything that can be made into a long strand can be knitted. As well as everything you can find in the shops you could knit with many other materials that you might have lying around.

You can shred fabric into strips and knit with that, although you need more fabric than you might imagine to knit a large item. I have seen people knitting with strips made from old carrier bags. This can be very colourful if you choose the right bags and can form an interesting part of a wall-hanging. A garment made from old carrier bags would not be very comfortable to wear but it would be waterproof.

Don't throw away your old tights. Cut them into strips and knit with them. I have even heard of people knitting jewellery, using fine coloured wires and silver filigree wire. Look out for anything that could become strips for knitting and try it out. You will never know what happens if you don't try.

WHERE TO BUY YARNS
Specialist yarn shops obviously offer the best range of yarns, though some are better than others. You should also investigate chain stores and department stores as well as any markets, mill shops and one-day sales. Mail order is another possibility.

HOW MUCH YARN TO BUY This is one of the trickiest problems when you are making up your own designs. Commercial patterns tell you how much to buy. There is always enough and often some left over.

It is best to get more yarn than you think you need. You can usually take back any complete balls you have left over. However, if you become an addicted knitter you will never want to return anything.

ESTIMATING QUANTITIES You need to have a rough idea of how much yarn you need. That can be difficult if you are using several different shades. One ball of each may be enough and, depending on the size of the ball, you might have a lot left over for use in the future. If you want very small amounts some manufacturers still make some 25 gram balls. For even smaller amounts look for tapestry wools which come in a huge range of colours but are expensive for anything other than very special use.

You will have to try to estimate as closely as you can. If your design has several squares the same, buy one ball of yarn and see how many squares you can knit with it. For example, if one ball knits five squares and you have to make 18 squares you will need four balls.

Because the yarn is sold by weight, thin ones weigh less than thick ones. The yarn in a ball of 4 ply is much longer than in the same weight ball of thicker yarn. You will not need as many balls if you are working in thin yarn.

If you manage to estimate fairly accurately for one part of your design, common sense should tell you whether you need more or less for other parts. Always get more than you need unless you are certain you can go back to the shop for more.

If the worst happens and you do run out of yarn before you've finished, don't worry about it. Adapt your design to suit the yarn available and pretend that was the way you always intended it to be. If you make the design look planned no one will know you had to change your mind.

If you work with oddments of yarn that have been collected over a period of time, as I often do, your design will have to undergo constant revision to make best use of the materials available. Always be prepared to adapt, or even abandon, your original ideas. You can make good use of any interesting yarns you may have even if they are in small amounts.

COLLECTING YARNS You do not have to wait until you want to knit something before you start buying yarns. Keep your eyes open for interesting oddments all the time and pick up anything you know you can blend with other yarns.

Build up a collection but don't be too fixed in your ideas of what should go together. I arrange my yarns in broad colour groups but frequently find myself moving balls from one bag to another when I look at them with different ideas in mind.

See-through carrier bags are very useful for storing yarns because they can give an overall effect of colours you have put together and you can often find the ball you want without having to empty everything out.

You may well find that you will keep a particular yarn for years, either because you become attached to it and don't want to use it, or because it never seems quite right to use. Eventually it could be the very thing you need.

These interesting yarns can often be enough to spark off ideas. One ball can provide inspiration for a whole garment.

You can have as many different colours as you want in your design. The usual way of changing the colours is to use a new one for each new shape. You could also break off one yarn at the end of a row to bring in a new one. These are not the only ways to introduce a range of colours. You can use yarn from various sources to make your own multi-coloured yarn, which can produce interesting effects.

USING LEFTOVERS Make your own ball of yarn from lots of bits. You have to use yarns of similar thickness or you will get thick and thin patches in your knitting. You can use as many shades and textures as you like. The colour combinations can be subtle or striking - it's up to you. This is a good way to use up any oddments that are not big enough to make a whole shape. If you take care to create an interesting overall effect no one will realise you have been using up leftovers.

If you don't have enough bits already there are various ways of acquiring more. Ask other knitters to give you all their bits. Anything over a metre in length will be long enough. You might be able to come to some arrangement whereby you swap leftovers.

SECONDS Sometimes you might be lucky enough to find yarn from well-known manufacturers marked as seconds. It is difficult to notice anything wrong with this yarn. The fault could be minor imperfections in the dye that was used or the yarn could have knots in it. Neither of these faults would cause you any problem at all. Even noticeable shading is unimportant, and you are going to put knots into your own yarn.

MAKING YOUR YARN Decide on the effect you want to create and collect the appropriate yarn. Spread out everything you intend to use and choose yarns in any order to make the new ball. Make a tiny ball with the first colour. Break off that yarn and choose the next colour. Join together shades that look almost identical. Each individual change will be hard to see. Only when you look at the overall effect will you notice how many shades there are. Usually, the more shades you use the more interesting the finished effect.

Tie the two pieces together with a simple knot leaving tails of 4 or 5 cm so that both tails lie in the same

SUBTLE EFFECTS
If you intend to create a subtle effect you will have to search for lots of yarns in the same range of colours. There are hundreds of shades and textures to choose from, especially if you go to more than one shop. Find as many variations of shade and/or texture as you can. The more changes you have the less each one will be noticed.

Go to several shops and buy yarns made by different manufacturers to get a slight variation in shades. Variation of shade also occurs if you choose yarns in the same shade from the same manufacturer but with different fibre content. You can even get minute variations by buying yarn from different batches. The dye can vary a little from one batch to the next. Due to modern manufacturing conditions this is usually difficult to notice but all manufacturers warn that it is likely to happen so you should keep a lookout for the times when it does. You can often buy odd balls cheaply because they have been left over at the end of a dye batch.

direction. Continue winding and then break off again and tie on the next colour. Keep going until you have a large ball.

You must decide how long you want the pieces to be. If you are knitting short rows you may want short pieces but it's entirely up to you. Short pieces will always give you more variety of colours than longer ones. You will soon find out what works best. You can easily break the pieces again if you find they are too long when you start working. Vary the lengths of the pieces you use or your knitting will start to look like stripes that went wrong instead of a carefully planned design.

USING YOUR YARN
This yarn has many knots in it. All the books tell you that you should not join yarn in the middle of a row. **Ignore all conventional books.** Deal with the knots as you go along and they will not cause any problems.

You must be sure which is the back of your work and all the knots must be on that side. When you come to a knot, keep the knobbly bit and the tails at the back and for the next 6 or 7 stitches wrap the tails over the yarn you are working with before you knit each stitch. Do not use the tails to knit the stitches or you will make a bulge in the knitting. After a few stitches the tails will be firmly fixed in and the ends can be snipped off close to the knitting. Keep a pair of sharp scissors by you all the time. You will need them often.

Changing yarns in the middle of a row adds to the interesting colour combinations you are using. If the first stitch with the knot in it is not quite perfect it won't matter. Your eye will be distracted by the colour changes.

When you happen to be knitting on the wrong side and you come to a knot you will find that it is difficult to twist in the tails without them showing on the right side. Leave the tails until you reach the same place on the next row, on the way back, then treat them in exactly the same way, without pulling too tight.

If you are at the end of a right side row there is nowhere for the tails to go. Either twist them round the yarn before the last stitch on a few successive rows, or darn them in later.

You might find that the colours look even more mixed than you had expected. It depends on whether the colour changes on the back or the front.

ODDMENTS
When you do have to buy more it is often possible to buy odd balls quite cheaply. Most wool shops have a box or basket of oddments that may be the end of a particular batch of yarn, or have lost their bands, or got into a bit of a tangle.

When you are planning to make something in a particular range of shades you could ask the shopkeeper to save you any odd balls that turn up in those shades. Customers often bring back odd balls that are left over and the shopkeeper adds them to the oddments.

MAKING SHAPES

The secret of this type of design is getting each square to be exactly the size you want. If you follow the instructions for knitting a square you will be able to get the right size every time.

When you have decided on the size, draw your square on paper and use this outline, on a flat surface, to check the measurements of all your squares. Always go back to this outline, not a square you've already made, or you might find your squares getting progressively larger, or smaller.

Once you understand how to make a square to the correct size it is easy to adapt the method to make various other geometric shapes. Whatever yarn you are working with, whatever size needles you use, you will always produce the same shape. You will just need fewer rows if you are working with thick yarn, making shapes that grow quickly, than if you were working with thinner yarn.

On the next few pages there are examples of shapes you could make and instructions for making them. They are intended to give you ideas. You can combine aspects of different shapes and probably think of some original ones as well. When you are planning shapes the only essential point to remember is that they are meant to fit together, so the edges that are to be joined must be exactly the same length. If they are just slightly different your jumper will be affected in several places and will look messy.

Remember **you are not working to a particular tension.** You are always working with measurements, not numbers of stitches. Measure very, very carefully. Be accurate. Do not try to stretch pieces to fit. The extra time to knit another row or two will be time well-spent.

By the time you have worked through the shapes you will probably have noticed what is happening to make the shapes come out as they do. The rules are very simple and you can devise your own shapes once you understand them.

COMPLEX SHAPES There are also ways of making shapes that do not start from a single point, but they are only appropriate when you have already made a basic shape to build on. You need to learn some more knitting techniques, which will come later, on pages 68-71.

1. Always begin at a point.

2. Increase in the last stitch on every row to get a square corner.

3. Keep one side straight and increase in the last stitch on the other side to get 45°.

4. Starting from a wide shape, decrease at the end of every row and the sides come together to make a square corner.

5. Starting from a wide shape, keep one side straight and decrease at the other side to turn inwards by 45°.

6. Don't increase or decrease and you will have straight rows of knitting parallel to the row where you stopped shaping.

YOUR OWN SHAPES
It is a good idea to draw your shapes and work out which way the lines of knitting will run, to be sure the shape will go the way you want. You will only be working with small pieces so it won't be too disastrous if you get it wrong. If you do, pull the piece undone and start again. When you've got it right, make a note or sketch of how you made the shape so that you won't need to work it out again.

REVERSING SHAPES You have probably realised that you can get shapes the opposite way round from the ones you have already knitted by turning them over or turning them round. There are times when it is not satisfactory to turn shapes over and you will have to make the shapes the opposite way, by shaping opposite sides. Decide whether this is necessary before you begin each shape.

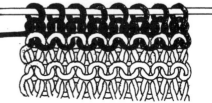

These drawings show what happens if you change yarn and then turn the shape over. You could choose either effect - one creates a clear line, the other gives a blurred change. This problem does not arise when your shape is only one colour.

COMBINATION SHAPE This shape can be made in sections to be joined together. Make one small triangle until you reach the widest part. Break off the yarn, leaving 10 - 15 cm. Keep the stitches on a stitch-holder or spare needle until you want them again. Make the other small triangles in the same way but do not break off the yarn at the end of the last one or put the stitches on a holder. To join the pieces, firstly knit across the stitches that are still on the needle, then knit across the other pieces using the same yarn.

Take care to get all the pieces with the right sides facing you. The tail of the yarn you broke off will be at the start of the stitches and should be twisted round the yarn you are working with before you knit each of the first 5 or 6 stitches of each set. This will keep the pieces tightly together and you can cut off the ends when they are secure. Complete the whole shape by decreasing at the end of every row.

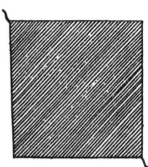

This is the basic square you have already knitted.

It is easy to see that the following shapes are closely related to your original squares. It may not be quite so easy to see how they evolve.

The instructions explain what to do. The fine lines on the drawings show the direction of the lines (rows) of knitting. The sizes will be up to you.

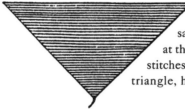

To make this triangle start in the same way as for knitting a square. Stop at the widest part and cast off all the stitches. (see page 73). You will have a triangle, half the size of your square.

This is a triangle with a straight piece of knitting attached to it. Start by making the triangle in the same way you made the first half of a square. When you reach the widest part, carry on knitting straight, without increasing or decreasing at the end of the rows. You can make the triangle whatever width you choose, and the straight section as long or short as you like. Cast off all the stitches when the straight part is long enough.

Here are two halves of a square with a straight piece of knitting in between. To make it, follow the instructions for knitting a square, up to the widest part, then knit straight, without increasing or decreasing, until the middle bit is the length you want. Finish the shape in the same way you finish a square, decreasing at the end of every row.

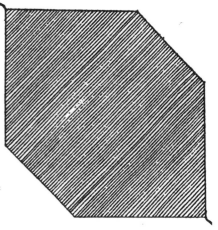

To make a rectangle, start in the same way as for making a square, until you reach the widest part. One side is then exactly the same as the side of the square while the other side does not turn inwards, it keeps going in the same direction. At the side that turns the corner you must decrease, like you do for a square. On the other side you must continue to increase in the same way that you have been doing. That side will carry on in the same straight line. You are now decreasing on one row, increasing on the next. You lose a stitch on one row and gain one on the next, so every two rows you will have the same number of stitches. When the rectangle has reached the length you want, complete the point by decreasing at the end of every row, as you do for a square.

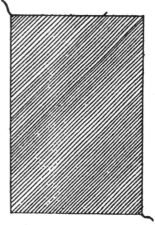

STRIPS Rectangles can be any length. They can become long strips, long enough to go all the way round a cardigan and meet at the centre front. Strips can also be used vertically. One strip can go right up the front of a jumper, over the shoulder, and down the back. A combination of long and shorter strips can make a whole garment. This does not involve as much sewing together as some of the other shapes.

ANGULAR SHAPES

All of the shapes described so far have at least one right angle (90°). Your shapes do not have to have square corners. It is just as easy to make corners that are half a right angle (45°). Some of the possibilities are shown here.

1. Two of these placed to face each other could make a square. The shape is half a square and has 45° angles at the top and bottom. One side of it is straight and has no shaping at all, the other is shaped in the same way as the side of the square. When you make it, decide which is to be the straight side and do not do any increasing or decreasing at that side. All the shaping is done at the other side. In the first half of the shape you must increase one stitch each time you reach that end of the knitting. After you have reached the widest part you must decrease each time you reach that end.

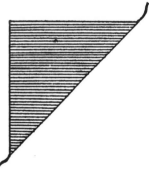

2. This is one half of shape 1 and is knitted in the same way. It has 45° angles at the two pointed corners and 90° at the other.

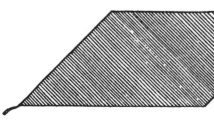

3. This parallelogram starts in the same way as shapes 1 and 2 until it reaches the widest part. Then the side that was being shaped continues straight, without any increasing or decreasing. The side that was straight starts to be shaped inwards by decreasing every time you reach that end.

4. This is another parallelogram and is like shape 3 with another piece in the middle. Begin in the same way as shapes 1, 2 and 3, keeping one side straight and increasing at the other. When you reach the widest part, both sides carry on without any shaping until you reach the part where you want to shape again. Then the side that was originally shaped continues straight and the side that was straight is turned inwards by decreasing each time you reach that end.

5. This is very similar to 4. The only difference is that you cast off all the stitches when the straight part is as long as you want.

6. This is shape 1 with a straight part in the middle. Begin in the way you started shape 1, knit straight for as long as you want and finish in the same way as you finished shape 1

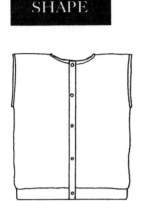

There are many alterations you might want to make to the basic jumper shape.

Make a back like before, make the front in two halves, join them together and you will have a waistcoat.

By adding sleeves the waistcoat becomes a cardigan or jacket. Make it longer and it can be a coat.

SLEEVE SHAPE You may want to alter the sleeves. The basic rectangle shape will give you very loose, baggy sleeves. This shape is ideal for some styles but you will sometimes want to change it as it is not always comfortable to have so much fabric flapping around.

You will have to decide what sort of sleeves you want. You can have whatever you like. Get ideas by trying on clothes you already have and copying the shape. It's your design, you must decide.

It is possible to change the top of your sleeve, but this is likely to interfere with the pattern on the front, back and sleeve tops. A straight loose-fitting top to a sleeve is acceptable for most designs if the lower part of the sleeve is more tailored. Focus your attention on making the sleeves an integral part of your design, rather than using complex shapes.

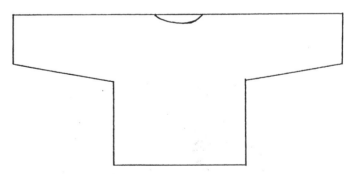

BOTTOM BANDS You can drastically alter the appearance by adding a bottom band that is tighter than the rest of your garment. When the band is the same size as the rest the whole shape will be straight. A tighter band, or a looser garment, will create a bloused effect. (Find out how to add bands on page 72.)

SLEEVE BANDS Garter

stitch is not very stretchy, so any band should be just loose enough to go over your hand or it will be too loose around the wrist.

Sleeves often have some fullness immediately above the band. They don't have to, it's up to you. A full sleeve could have twice as many stitches at the bottom of the sleeve as on the band. A less full sleeve would have one and a quarter or one and a half times the stitches on the band. The rest of the sleeve gradually gets wider to the straight edge at the top.

BUTTON BANDS If you are making a coat, jacket

or cardigan you will probably need fastenings. The simplest way to add them is on an extra band which you join on when the garment is almost finished. It is possible to make buttonholes, or other fastenings, in the main pieces as you go along, if you plan in advance. It takes a lot of mental effort to remember them when you are concentrating on making shapes. It is usually easier to wait until everything else is finished and then decide how many fastenings you need and where they should be.

TOP DOWNWARDS It is often easier to work

sleeves from the top downwards, possibly picking up stitches from the front and back of the garment.

Sleeves can be a continuation of the design covering the front and back. Working out from the centre, in all four directions, you are less likely to make a mistake because you can make the same section of each piece so you can be sure they are alike, or opposite, or whatever you intend.

As with the rest of your work you must keep looking and checking that what you are making is exactly what you want it to be. It is much easier to put right a small mistake just after you have made it than it is to undo a whole garment. Everyone makes mistakes, it is inevitable. The important part is recognising them as soon as possible.

I usually join pieces as I am going along, partly to be able to spot mistakes in the design or choice of colours, and partly because I like to see the design emerging and do not want to wait until all the individual pieces are finished.

MATCHING SLEEVES It is very easy to make a mistake with the direction of the design on the sleeves and get it all completely reversed, then find it won't fit either side.

Sometimes you will be making two identical sleeves, sometimes they will be a mirror image of each other, sometimes they will be completely different from each other.

It would be very unusual for the two sleeves to be different shapes from each other but even that is possible if that is what you want.

You can continue to make alterations to the basic shape, in any combination.

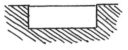

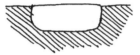

Draw the pieces

If your neck shapes, or any of your other pieces, are complex, draw them full-size on paper before you start. Check frequently to make sure you are achieving the right shape.

This is a good, successful way to get it right. If you want to be more scientific about it you will need to look at each piece of shaping individually and apply some logical thought to the problem.

Remember that the two sides of your garment are mirror images. You may need to take this into account in your shaping and not make pairs of identical pieces. If you are an experienced knitter you will be quite used to knitting mirror-image pieces as you do for the two fronts of most cardigan or jacket patterns. It helps if you assemble the pieces as you make them, so that you can see as soon as anything starts to go wrong.

NECK SHAPING If the front of your basic jumper is made from a rectangle the same as the back, you will be able to stitch the two rectangles together and leave an opening for your head. You will have a jumper with a straight neck (A slash neck). This is the simplest shape but you can make a more interesting neckline.

Sometimes it is extremely easy to make a small v-neck, by knitting a triangle instead of a square. A v-neck is fairly easy to create in most designs. Look at the drawings of variations on a basic square and see if one of them, or part of one, could be strategically placed to make the neck.

Other shapes are more complicated and depend on the direction of the knitting where the shaping occurs. If possible, work the shaping in a small shape which can be joined on later. If you should happen to make a mistake, it would be easy to start the piece again.

SHAPING As you have already learnt, when you made variations on a basic square, decreasing one stitch on alternate rows will bring in the edge of the work by 45°. Decreasing less often means the side of your shape will not come in so quickly and the angle will be bigger. Decreasing more often makes the slope come in more quickly. Similarly, increasing on alternate rows makes the side of the shape point outwards by an extra 45°. More, or less, frequent increases will change that angle.

Very often you will already be shaping a piece when you have to start shaping for the garment. The extra shaping usually has to be in addition to the shaping for the piece.

When drastic shaping is needed, cast on or cast off a few stitches at the start of a row. If the shaping is less severe you can increase or decrease on every row instead of on alternate rows. You can also decrease extra stitches by knitting three or more together instead of just two. Only do this if there is no other way. It is better to knit two together on every row than knit three together on alternate rows because it gives a smoother edge.

This sounds complicated but it isn't as difficult as it seems if you know exactly what each piece should look like. Always knit as closely as possible to the shape you want. Do not try to stretch or push pieces into place when they're finished.

Experience will tell you how often to increase or

decrease. You can use any combination to make your shape but you will need to repeat the actions less often with thicker yarn.

MEASUREMENTS
For all alterations you will need rather more measurements than you have used so far. On page 100 you will find a size chart of the type used by many commercial pattern designers. It gives average measurements of many parts of a garment. Use it for reference but also make a note of the measurements of any of your own clothes and try to copy them when you want to.

The firms who produce patterns for "designer knitwear" do not use these charts because they treat every new style differently.

There should be books in your library which will tell you more about taking measurements. Some of them are excellent and should be used as a source of ideas.

The best way to decide on the size is to copy it from other clothes that you like. You can combine the shape of the neck of your T-shirt with the sleeves of a jumper and the length of your bath robe. The shape can be as individual as the patchwork design but you must take care if you are creating something of a different thickness from the original. An enormously baggy T-shirt might be comfortable, whereas the same size in a chunky jacket could be too heavy and bulky.

Keep the shape simple. A complex shape would be lost in an intricate multi-coloured pattern, so there is little point in spending a great deal of time and effort constructing a complicated garment shape.

Many knitted garments come from the same basic shape. Sometimes the sleeves are wider or longer, the jumper can be longer or shorter, the front can be split in half to make a cardigan– it is still basically the same shape whether it is for a man, woman or child. Forget all the rules. Adapt the shape in any way that suits you.

THE SCIENTIFIC APPROACH
Try to work out how many stitches you will need to have on the needle by the time you get to the end of the piece, and how many rows you should knit to get there. Work out how often you need to increase or decrease to get to the right number before you finish all the rows.

In ordinary knitting it is easy to give instructions for shaping because you are almost always knitting in the same direction and the same rules will always apply. With this method it is possible, but unlikely, for each piece to be knitted in a different direction, so you will need a different method for each one.

If you would like a little more guidance on the number of increasings or decreasings to create a particular angle you could consult **Calculations**, but that is no substitute for drawing your own shape and knitting to match it.

TIDYING UP YOUR SHAPING
The shaping is often not quite as crucial as you might imagine. A neck which is almost right will usually be pulled into a perfect-looking shape by the addition of a neckband.

Even a shallow v-neck made up of three straight edges will be quite rounded if it has a band made from one continuous row of stitches.

A completely square neck will look slightly rounded when it has just one extra row knitted on stitches picked up from the edges.

Take care not to make the original neck opening too tight. If it is in a jumper you won't be able to get it over your head. In a cardigan it might be uncomfortable to button up. It is better to make the opening too loose and close it up later by adding a band. (See Cheating, page 80.)

PICKING UP STITCHES

You should always start work with a basic square somewhere in the design and this should act as your reference point for all calculations.

There are many occasions when you will want to pick up stitches along the edge of a piece you have already made so that you can continue knitting in another direction. Once you have mastered this technique and discovered the advantages you will find more and more ways to use it.

HOW MANY STITCHES? Some basic maths is all you need to work out the number of stitches you should pick up. If you want more information about the mathematics refer to **Calculations**.

COMBINING METHODS If the new row of stitches spans more than one of your original shapes, and they were knitted in different directions, you may find yourself using more than one method of calculation. Treat each part individually, pick up the right number from each bit and knit them into one long row.

CHANGING ANSWERS These calculations will give numbers for a new piece of knitting that will lie flat with the rest of your work. If you do not want it all to lie flat you can change the number of stitches to suit your purpose.

To make a band that is tighter than the other knitting, pick up fewer stitches. To make the new piece frill out from the rest, pick up extra stitches.

CALCULATING - METHOD 1 I shall assume that you are using the same type of yarn for picking up the stitches as you have been using for the piece already made and that you want the next piece to lie flat. If you are using yarn of a different thickness you will have to adjust the number of stitches. Thicker yarn will need less, thinner yarn will need more.

You must remember how many stitches there were on the needle at the widest part of your square. This number is the 'length' of the diagonal of your square and you need to find the 'length' of the side of the square.

Divide the length of the diagonal by 1.4 to get the number of stitches for the side. You will not always get a whole number so you should use the nearest whole number. One stitch either way won't make much difference, unless you are working in very thick yarn. You might want to choose the nearest even number in some circumstances, or an odd number in others. Remember that the side is shorter than the diagonal so it will have fewer stitches.

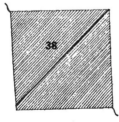

Example
The diagonal has 38 stitches.
Divide by 1.4
Answer = 27.124
Pick up 27 stitches
If you want an even number
pick up 28.

CALCULATING - METHOD 2

If you don't have a basic square to work from you might need another way of working out the number of stitches. You will need a piece of garter stitch in the thickness of yarn that you intend to use for picking up the new stitches.

Use two pins to mark 10 cm on the width of garter stitch. Count how many stitches are between the pins. Count either the bottom loops of the stitches, or the top loops, not both. Divide by 10 to find out how many stitches are needed for each centimetre. Multiply the answer by the number of centimetres you want to make, rounding to the nearest whole number. This will tell you how many stitches to pick up.

Example
10 cm is 16 stitches
Divide by 10
Answer = 1.6 (stitches per centimetre)
I want to make 13 cm
Multiply 1.6 by 13
Answer = 20.8
Pick up 21 (or 20) stitches

CALCULATING - METHOD 3

Picking up stitches where you have previously cast off needs no calculation, only careful counting to make sure you pick up all the stitches you had before. Pick up both loops of each stitch where they lie along the edge of the knitting.

In a multi-coloured garment this will hardly show, so it can be used for lengthening knitting.

CALCULATING - METHOD 4

When you want to pick up across the ends of the rows of a straight section of knitting, count the ridges and pick up one stitch for each ridge.

CURVED EDGES

Most picking up will be along straight edges. Curved edges are made up of a series of straight sections and can be treated as such .

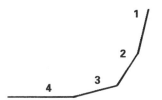

Alternatively, decide how many stitches you need along the whole curve by comparing it with another area of your work. Divide the curve into equal sections with safety pins, divide the stitches needed by the number of sections and pick up the right number of stitches in each section to give the total.

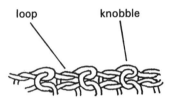

HOW TO PICK UP STITCHES

loop   knobble

KNOBBLES AND LOOPS
Look at a piece of garter stitch knitting and you will see that it is made up of ridges and furrows. At the edge of the piece you should be able to see a knobble at the end of each ridge and a tiny loop at the end of each furrow. These knobbles and loops are where you are going to pick up the new stitches.

The same principles apply whatever the angle between your rows and the edge of the knitting. The loops can be difficult to see if you have a lot of increasing or decreasing.

Now that you know how many stitches you need, you have to decide precisely where to pick them up.

COUNTING THE STITCHES Study your piece of knitting carefully to see how you can space the number of new stitches evenly along the edge. The best bits to pick up are the knobbles at the end of the ridges because they are usually firmer and easier to find, so start by counting the knobbles. There probably won't be as many knobbles as you want stitches so you will have to pick up some stitches from loops as well. You are unlikely to need one from every loop so space them out: picking up knobble, knobble, loop, knobble, knobble, knobble, loop often works out about right. Count carefully before you begin and adjust if necessary.

PICKING UP STITCHES ALONG AN EDGE
Follow the drawings to see how to pick up the stitches along the edge of your existing piece of knitting, having read the following notes first.

Always work with the right side of the work facing you. Count the row where you are picking up the stitches as the first row of your new piece, it will form the bottom half of the first ridge.

Work all along the piece, very close to the edge, picking up one stitch wherever you have decided you need one. Sometimes this can be quite awkward, especially if your knitting is very tight or you are trying to pull a thick yarn through a thinner one. Be patient at this stage and try to pick up each knobble in exactly the same way and each loop alike so that your new row looks neat and even.

You may notice several places where you could insert the needle in the knitting and still be right on the edge. It doesn't matter which bit you choose as long as the work has no thick ridges on the back, no stringy loops on the front, and lies flat when you open it out. Choose the way you think looks best and stick to it for the entire garment.

MORE STITCHES THAN KNOBBLES Never try to pick up two stitches from the same loop or knobble, because one of the stitches will disappear on the next row and leave you short. On the very rare occasion when you need more stitches than you have loops and knobbles, pick up a stitch from every loop and knobble, work out how many more you need and increase evenly by that number on the next row.

Take care to pick up stitches right to the end of the line where you want the new piece to go. It is very easy to miss the end of the line, especially when it is at a corner of the shape. Sometimes the corner stitches have been pulled together more than others. Pull the edges of the shape gently to make sure you have counted the ends of all the rows. If you miss the corners or do not pick up enough stitches there, your shapes will not fit together properly and you will spoil your carefully worked out geometric design.

WHERE TO PICK UP STITCHES
You can pick up a row of stitches anywhere you want but it must be along a straight edge or the work will not lie flat. The method is equally suitable for very small pieces and large sections, like sleeves. As you use the idea you will find more and more places where you could do it.

When you have got the stitches on your needle you should be able to use the shaping techniques you have already learned to produce more complicated shapes than those you have previously created.

Now that more of your shapes are beginning with a row of stitches it is more likely that you will also be ending with a row and you will need to cast off several stitches at a time (see page 73 for how to do this).

KEEPING SHAPES FLAT
Picking-up and casting-off rows are places where keeping shapes flat can be a problem. In both cases you can overcome the difficulty by using needles a size or two larger than those used for the rest of the work. Use them for just the one row and be sure to remember to change back again.

Casting off at the end of any piece of knitting can be done on either side. The choice may affect the way the piece lies. The work will look better if you decide which side to use and do the same throughout the garment; differences can be quite noticeable.

Try both sides for casting off. I always use the wrong side because I think it gives a neater edge for joining pieces together later. It is purely a matter of personal preference and you can vary from garment to garment.

Work along the edge of the knitting, with the right side facing you, using only one needle until you have picked up all the stitches.
Put the needle through the first knobble (or loop) where you want to pick up a stitch. Wrap the yarn round the needle in the same way as knitting a stitch. The other end of the yarn will be loose so take care not to pull it right through.

Pull the loop of yarn through the knobble (or loop) to form the first stitch on the needle.

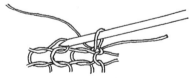

Put the needle through the next knobble (or loop) and make the next stitch the same way. Continue until you have all the stitches.

Rule for decreasing

Divide the number of stitches you have by the number you need to lose, ignoring any remainders. If the answer is 3, every third stitch has to go. If the answer is 4, every fourth stitch has to go.

Example

If you have picked up 50 stitches and only want 40 for the band, then 10 will have to go. There are 5 tens in 50 so in each group of 5 stitches one will have to go. You will have to knit two stitches together once in each group of 5. Knit three stitches and then knit two together. Continue like this right across the row. Each group of 5 will have turned into a group of 4 and you will be left with 10 groups of 4, which is 40.

Bands can be knitted separately and then stitched onto a garment. I knit all bands by picking up stitches and knitting out from the garment. This gives a much neater finish and saves the time and effort of stitching up.

Commercial patterns usually begin each piece with the bands, but if you work them afterwards their effect on the garment can be seen at once.

The bands might be for the front, bottom, sleeves, neck, or pocket tops of a cardigan or jumper. They could be the waistband or hem of a skirt, the brim of a hat, or anywhere else an edging is necessary to complete a design, add extra length or weight, or neaten edges. The method is always the same as picking up a few stitches for a small piece.

Work out the number of stitches in the same way as for small pieces. If you want the band to be a little firmer than the rest of the garment, use needles one or two sizes smaller.

Decide how many stitches you need for the band, knit as many rows as you need and cast off very loosely. If your casting off is too tight it will pull the garment out of shape and it will be uncomfortable to wear. If the edge does not stretch enough, undo the casting off and try again with larger needles. Keep trying different sizes until you get what you want. You may need to use several sizes larger. If you are not sure whether it is loose enough, make it looser still. Do not spoil the whole garment for the sake of a few more minutes to do the casting off again.

Very loose casting off occasionally causes problems if it is on the edge of a shape or somewhere else where you need to pick up stitches. If it is too loose it may leave a row of holes at the edge of the shape.

Loose casting off is not needed on a curved neckband. It should be cast off with the same needles you have been using, so it continues to curve inwards. If the band is too tight, cast off using the smallest needles that will allow it to go over your head.

SHAPED BANDS A deep band around the bottom of a garment might need to taper in gently. You could start with the needles from the rest of the knitting, knit a few rows, change to the next size thinner, knit a few rows, change to the next thinner, knit a few more rows and cast off loosely. When you change needles gradually it changes the shape of the band.

The shape of any band can be altered in this way. Turn your neckband into a shaped collar; shape the waist section of a jumper or skirt - use this method anywhere you would like gentle shaping.

SLEEVE BANDS Sleeve bands are sometimes different from other bands because there can be much more fullness to deal with. The band might need to be smaller than the bottom of the main part of the sleeve. If it is going to be close-fitting, use another piece of knitting to measure the smallest size that will slip over your hand.

There may be a lot of ridges and loops on the bottom of the piece of knitting where you are picking up the stitches and you might not want that many on the sleeve band. If you pick up only the number of stitches you need for the band, you may find bits of the sleeve stick out, so you should pick up one stitch from every knobble and count how many you have got. On the next row you will have to 'lose' some stitches so work out how many have to go. For each stitch you need to lose you will have to knit two stitches together somewhere on the row.

All books about knitting will show you how to cast off. Almost all of them will show casting off in stocking stitch, not garter stitch. The methods are exactly the same.

There are many ways of casting off. If you know any others, try them and see which looks best.

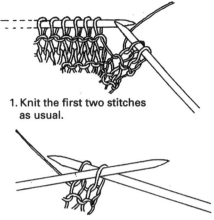

1. Knit the first two stitches as usual.

Use the point of the left hand needle to lift the first stitch over the second and off the needles.

There is now one stitch left on the needle. Knit the next stitch. Lift the new first stitch over the other. Continue along the row until one stitch remains.

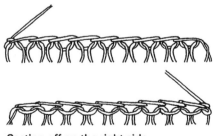

Cut the yarn and fasten off by pulling the end through the remaining loop.

Casting off on the right side gives a very smooth line of stitches; casting off on the wrong side creates a more uneven edge. Use whichever you prefer.

JOINING SHAPES

Other ways of joining with knitting The joins can become a more obvious part of your design. If you pick up stitches along the edge of a shape and cast them off again loosely on the next row you will make a very neat edge. Do the same on all edges and your shapes will have a narrow border that can be used to stitch them together. You could use a contrasting colour for the borders. This is a more time-consuming way of joining shapes but it can look very effective. It can also serve the purpose of supporting any pieces that might be a bit floppy on the edge. It is also useful if you have difficulty joining together pieces of different thicknesses. The border could make the shapes slightly larger although the difference is usually negligible.

Each garment will be different when it comes to joining the pieces because there will be a variety of shapes to join. Plan the making up as carefully as you plan the design. See if you can make a few small pieces into a larger one before you have to join them onto another large one.

It will probably be helpful to spread out all the pieces in their final position and leave them there until you need each one. I often use a padded, squared board for this because the pieces can be pinned in place and the squares can be used to check measurements.

Do not rush this stage. Good designing and knitting are easily spoiled by careless joining.

JOINING WITH KNITTING Knitting can be used in a variety of ways to join your pieces. You can knit pieces together as you go along, in two different ways. One of these methods is described on pages 68-72. It is used for picking up a row of stitches, of any length, to start knitting a new shape.

Use this, and the method described here, to join shapes while you are still making them.

PICKING UP SINGLE STITCHES The times when you can use this way of picking up stitches are limited but it can save much measuring and counting.

It joins the shape you are knitting to one you have already knitted, as you go along, by picking up one stitch from the edge of the old shape instead of making an extra stitch at the end of the current row.

When the shape you are knitting is to have the same number of rows as the one from which you are picking up, you simply pick up the knobble at the end of each row to make the extra stitch on your needle, instead of knitting twice into the end stitch.

If the shapes are of different thicknesses or at different angles, you will need to work out which stitches on the old shape you should take.

It works best when the two shapes being joined have 90° angles and the shape you want to join to is on the left of the one to be knitted. You can work into the front of the piece and be sure that it will be neat, unlike working from the back. With fluffy or textured yarns you probably won't even be able to see the join. Try it to see if the appearance is acceptable.

You can work a few stitches like this or go right

across your jumper. You must plan and check these joins even more carefully than any others or you might not notice a mistake until the end and would have to pull the whole piece undone.

KNITTING TWO ROWS TOGETHER

Another technique you might like to try involves knitting two lots of stitches, on two different needles, together. This is not easy but can be extremely useful if you want to make an almost invisible join.

You must have exactly the same number of stitches on each of the two pieces you want to join.

Hold the two needles in your left hand with the right sides of the shapes facing each other. (This assumes that you knit the right-handed way.) Knit together one stitch from the front needle and one from the back. Do this all along the row, casting off as you go You have to take great care not to drop any stitches. It might be easier to slip all the stitches on to a circular needle, taking them alternately from the two needles and then knitting them together, but it is still awkward to do as the stitches are very close together. You can also simplify the process slightly by knitting the stitches together on one row and casting off on the next. This will look the same on the outside but create a little ridge inside.

This method is useful for seams like shoulders as it has the effect of holding in place a seam that would be likely to drop. In some places you could find it tightens the seam too much, in which case you might have to use a needle several sizes larger than those you have been using.

JOINING WITH CROCHET

Crochet is often recommended as a way of joining. It can be a fairly quick process and it is easy to match pieces as it is done from the right side and you can see what you are doing. I have not managed to find a way of doing it that does not make the join lie to one side or the other. If a join is off-centre it ruins the accuracy of the mathematical shapes. If you are experienced at crochet you may be able to find a way round this problem.

Crochet can produce a bold, decorative finish which could be a feature of your design. If you would like to learn how to do it, borrow a book from the library.

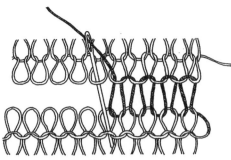

Grafting or weaving
This is another technique which can only be used when you have two equal rows of stitches that have not been cast off. The two rows of stitches are placed flat and pointing towards each other. The weaving imitates the pattern of the stitches and is done with the large blunt-ended needle you use for sewing up. Use a length of yarn long enough to complete the row and try to work at the same tension as the knitting. Pull the knitting needles out of the stitches as you come to them or you might lose some.

Decorative joins
The joins can become a feature if you work from the right side and oversew with a contrasting yarn. You can buy balls of ribbon from your wool shop to use in many decorative ways, as well as ordinary knitting.

If you are good at embroidery the stitching doesn't have to be so basic. There are several embroidery stitches that will stay flat when used for joins.

Using a sewing machine
Stitching up can also be done with a sewing machine, but you need to produce a flat edge-to-edge join and this is not easy unless you are very experienced. It is probably better to stitch by hand so that you can keep a careful check on your accuracy, which is vital when you are working with geometric shapes.

FASTENINGS

Buttons can add the finishing touch to anything you make and need to be chosen with care. Make them an integral part of your design.

BUYING BUTTONS

There is a huge range of buttons available if you shop around. Buying the exact number you need from a shop that sells them individually is often more economical than buying complete cards, when you may end up with some left over.

Look out for charity shops that sell the buttons they have removed from clothes that were not good enough to sell. These are usually cheap and can be very interesting if they have come off old clothes.

Always cut off the buttons from any clothes that you throw away. The buttons almost always outlive the fabric. If you keep them long enough you will eventually find a use for them.

The colour you go looking for may not always be the one that works best. Take the finished garment with you when you go to buy the buttons, or a sample of the yarns you used, and try to look at the overall effect, not individual shades.

Keep an eye open for interesting shapes. Square and triangular buttons can sometimes be found. In some shops you will find an assortment of 'children's buttons' which can include brightly coloured, unusual shapes.

COVERING BUTTONS There are different types of button that you can cover for yourself. You can buy metal or plastic shapes which are intended to be covered with fabric. If you have suitable fabric you could use it to cover these shapes or knit your own fabric to cover the buttons. Experiment to see what works with your yarn.

This is one time you might want to knit in stocking stitch, because it is smoother and finer than garter stitch, and the only time you can iron your knitting. You will be making very small pieces so it won't matter if you ruin them and have to start again. Pressing with a damp cloth and hot iron will probably make the knitting very limp and easy to mould. Washing in extremely hot water might thicken it and make a denser cover.

Read the button pack to find out how big your covers have to be. Use the thinnest needles you can manage to knit with and make a firm fabric to cover the buttons. If you think the fabric is still going to stretch, or show the shiny part of the button, add a backing of lining or interfacing first.

If the cover is too thick for the back to fit on the button, just gather the fabric behind the button and fasten it securely.

DORSET BUTTONS You may come across other buttons that are meant to be covered with yarn. They usually come in a pack, look like clear plastic circles with holes in and are sometimes called Dorset buttons. You wrap wool round the holes in a variety of ways. The pack will give you a few ideas and you should be able to use them to make buttons to match your cardigan.

A similar effect can be created with plastic curtain rings. Wrap yarn round and round and then stitch across the centre in various patterns. Avoid using brass ones as they may not wash well.

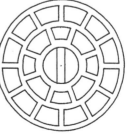

MAKING BUTTONS Buttons can be made from modelling material that can be hardened in the oven. You can mix colours and create shapes to match your cardigan. Remember to put holes in the shapes, or shanks on the back, before you harden them. Shanks are quite difficult to make and must be firmly attached or you will lose your buttons. The holes in flat buttons have to be surprisingly large, especially if you are going to stitch them on with the yarn from your knitting.

You could also try making buttons with wood. Evenly-shaped round ones can be sliced off a length of dowel, or create other interesting shapes from any off-cuts you can find. Wooden buttons need to be removed before washing or dry-cleaning.

BUTTONHOLES When you look in other knitting books you will find many ways of making buttonholes. I find that the hole created if you put the yarn over the needle and knit two together, so that you still have the same number of loops, is usually adequate and quite neat. Experiment to see which side of the knitting you prefer to do this. I like the holes to lie between the ridges of the knitting.

With thick yarns you get quite a large hole. In finer yarns you may need to use another method of making the holes. It depends on the thickness of the yarn and the size and shape of the buttons.

Have as many holes as you like to hold the garment together without looking cluttered. If possible work out their positions so they follow through the geometric lines of your shapes. On most bought garments and patterns the holes are evenly spaced. They don't have to be - it's up to you. Put them where you think they look good, remembering that they need to be functional.

POPPERS Look for decorative poppers that are put on with a special tool, which usually comes in the pack. There is less variety than with buttons but there are some interesting finishes that you wouldn't find in buttons.

Poppers tend to make a jacket look more casual. If they are appropriate to your design, try them but make sure you fix them securely. They may not grip as well on knitting as they do on other fabrics if you are not strong enough to press them hard. Give them extra stability by putting a small piece of non-fraying fabric behind the knitting where each popper is fixed.

Other fastenings
You can fasten your garment in other ways. You could use a zip, which has to be the open-ended type if you want your cardigan to open all the way down the front.

In the shops there are other types of fastenings, such as toggles, which fasten on with cord, or frogs, which are made from twisted decorative braid.

Invent your own fastenings. Keep your eyes open, see what you could fix to your cardigan that would hold it together. Do not use anything sharp and remember that whatever you use has to be washable or has to be removed each time you wash the garment.

FINISHINGS

SMOOTHING JOINS
Never iron or steam your garment. You will flatten the ridges and ruin it. Ignore any instructions about blocking and pressing that you might find on the ball bands or in other books about knitting. **Garter stitch should never be pressed** and should not need blocking. It should not need pulling into shape because you have knitted exactly the shapes you need and they should have stayed flat.

You might find that where you have joined two pieces together they do not lie as flat as they should. Lay the garment flat in a place where it can be left for some time and spray it. Do this on the floor or a table, or use a large padded board which can easily be moved or put outside to dry.

Use a spray, like those used for spraying plants, to spray your garment with cold water. Dampen it in the area where you need to smooth it, then gently pat into shape and leave until completely dry. Do not flatten the stitches; it is impossible to restore them if you do.

If you have been joining the pieces together as you have been making them, there is probably little to do to complete the garment. Join any remaining seams, darn in any ends, and you will be ready to add the finishing touches.

SHOULDERS Depending on the direction of your knitting, the garment could feel rather stretchy across the shoulders. If this happens it needs some support to stop it pulling out of shape. It should be strengthened with a non-stretchy tape inside the shoulders.

The tape should be strong enough to hold the knitting and fine enough not to show through.

Pat the garment back into its proper shape and carefully measure the length of tape needed to support the shoulder. It should start at the neckband or collar. It does not need to go into the sleeve but should stop at a point that will not make it obtrusive in your design.

Pin the tape in position, without stretching the shoulder. Tack if you think it will not stay in position while you sew.

Stitch firmly through the garment and the tape, either by hand, using a strong matching thread, or, even better, using a small zigzag stitch on a sewing machine. If you do this carefully it will not be noticed, as it will look like part of your design.

It is easier if you can stitch the tape in while the garment can still be opened flat.

Other seams should not need any support. If your garment does start to drop slightly it is unlikely that it will be only the seams that are dropping. If you put tape on the seams gravity will still act on the rest of the knitting and you will end up with a scalloped edge where the seams are held up and the rest drops down.

Unless you have knitted it too loosely your garment should not stretch. If it does you can leave it and pretend that was the length you wanted it to be, or you can alter it, after reading the suggestions on pages 80-82.

SHOULDER PADS The appearance of the shoulders can be altered by the addition of shoulder pads. They come in several shapes and styles. They do not have to be enormous, or noticeable, to improve the hang of your garment. Try different styles to see the effect they have.

You can make your own, from a commercial paper pattern, from wadding of various types, or from knitting. Knit them in the yarn of the garment and they will certainly not show through. Work with two or three strands together to make them more bulky, or use varying thicknesses to create the shaping. The easiest design to use is a square folded diagonally.

Decide on the position for your pads by wearing your garment and asking someone else to put them in for you. It is difficult to do this on your own because they move as you move your arms to reach them. Once you are satisfied that they look right and feel comfortable, pin them in place. Turn the garment inside out and stitch them in so that the stitching does not show on the outside.

Most shoulder pads have to be stitched in but you can also buy pads that do not have to be fixed. They just sit on your shoulder, under layers of clothes. They work surprisingly well but are a little inconvenient if you use them under your coat or cardigan and then decide to take it off.

TRIMMINGS Even when the garment is 'finished' you can continue to add more decoration to it. If you planned it carefully you will probably be quite happy with the results but there are many extra finishes that could be added.

You can pick up stitches again on the outside and knit extra bits and flaps and leave them hanging loose, stitch them down, twist them and stitch them, or anything else you fancy. Add a fringe or tassels, either at the edge or to create a yoke effect. Add beads, fur, feathers, braid, ribbon, or anything else that appeals to you.

Knitted garments can be effectively decorated with fabric paints and crayons. Look in your local craft shop to see what is available. Most products will not mention knitting as an appropriate use. Don't let that put you off. If you are not sure what will happen, knit a small sample and test on that first.

Embroider over your design with contrasting yarn, following the shape of the stitches, or in a completely different direction. If you carefully follow the shape of the existing stitches you can change the colour of an area where you have made a mistake or changed your mind.

Patches of fabric can be applied to the garment. There are many ways of doing this. Look in books about appliqué and embroidery for ideas of how to do it. When using other fabrics with knitting you will usually need to finish the fabric so it won't fray.

Take care not to distort the knitting when you stitch anything else to it.

This might be a good time to think about making one of your experimental garments as a mixture of fabric and knitted patchwork. This is outside the scope of this book but with a little inventiveness you should be able to find ways of doing it. Go to the library and look in books that have anything to do with any sort of fabric. Do not fall into the trap of believing that methods cannot be transferred from one fabric to another. Your knitting is only another type of fabric. **Ignore all the rules** and try ideas for yourself.

There are many, many ways of adding to your garment. Use them all with caution. Your design is unique. It may not need further embellishment.

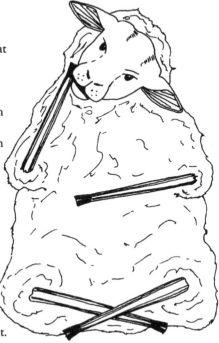

CHEATING

If all else fails and you can't work out a design or things do not go according to plan - cheat! Cheat with conviction and no one will ever know it wasn't part of your original plan. It's your design. Adapt and alter it at any stage in the proceedings.

You are bound to meet problems. New difficulties arise with every new idea. The easiest option is to give up and try something simpler. Don't. There is always some way round a problem. My ideas are not ideal solutions, merely different ways of looking at situations and, hopefully, turning disadvantages into assets.

MAKING A DESIGN FIT If you can't make the design fit you could change the dimensions of your garment a little. Think about the effect this would have. It may be the ratio between width and length that prevents you doing what you have in mind. Any change in the length might be very important to you whereas an extra couple of centimetres in the width would not be noticed and might give the proportions you want.

Think about all the implications of any alterations you make. Solving one problem could create others. For example, a looser body might make the sleeves drop down further so they would not have to be as long. You can overcome this problem by starting them at the top, knitting downwards and stopping when they are long enough. This is the opposite way from most commercial patterns.

REPOSITIONING THE DESIGN If you really wanted the design on the back to be repeated on the front, and then you find it is too big to fit, could you make it wrap round from front to back instead?

Try centring the design on the neck, instead of centre back or centre front. Your head would come through the centre of the design and it could look like a yoke, spreading down the sleeves as well as the front and back.

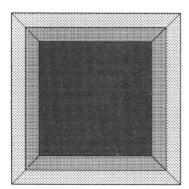

FRAMING THE DESIGN If your design is too small you might be able to rescale it. The other easy answer is to put it in a 'frame'. Pick up stitches, as though you were knitting a flat band, along each of the edges in turn. Knit as many rows as you need to make the panel the size you want. The frame can be plain and simple, with square or mitred joins at the corners, or it can be very ornate. You can use gold yarn to make a picture frame if you really want to.

LENGTHENING THE GARMENT When the
main part of your design is based on a square you may
find that you can make it wide enough but not long
enough. If this is the case add strips only to the top and
bottom.

A band added to the bottom may be enough to give
all the length you needed. However, there are other
advantages of having plain straight knitting at the top of
your design. It looks good because it creates a plain
section across the shoulder area. It is also useful
because it can take in all the area that includes the neck
shaping. If the shaping of the pieces at the neck is very
awkward, avoid the problem by putting all the shaping
in the plain section.

CUT AND SEW Many books about knitting
machines explain how to 'cut and sew'. This should
really be called sew and cut because you must make
sure all the knitted stitches are firmly stitched together
before you take the scissors to them.

You must use a sewing machine but it does not
matter if you are not experienced; all you have to do is
follow a line.

Use this method only if there is no other way of
shaping the pieces and only where it will not be seen. It
is ideal for knitting machine users because they can
work much faster if they don't have to stop to shape.
When you are knitting by hand it wastes your time
knitting parts you are going to throw away. If you have
to shape in this way, knit the smallest pieces that can be
used to make your shape.

Look at the diagram of a squared sleeve to get an
idea of the way you can minimise the amount of
knitting.

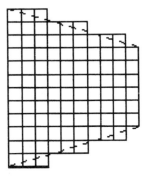

If possible, shape all the squares at the sides of the
sleeves to the exact sizes needed. If you can't do that,
think carefully about the precise slope of the sides so
you can make the minimum number of pieces. Do not
skimp on the number of squares because you will not be
happy with the results, but don't do any more than you
have to.

If you are not sure how full you want your sleeves to
be, make them bigger than you need and decide later
where to put the seam.

Decide where the seam is going to be and mark it
on the knitting. You could use chalk or tacking stitches
or special marker pens

Use a small zigzag stitch and sew along the line,

making sure that both ends are fastened off securely. Stitch again with the new line of stitching touching the other, slightly nearer to the edge you are going to cut away.

Now cut away the part you don't want. Use sharp scissors and take care not to cut the sewing. The knitting will not unravel unless you cut the stitching. As well as the waste piece of knitting, lots of little bits will fall off. They are messy but unimportant. Stitch the sleeve together with backstitch.

When you have tried the idea on a straight edge, try a curved neck. When you have finished it might look a bit untidy and not lie flat. Push it back into shape and cover up the messy edge by picking up stitches and knitting a band. There will be no knobbles to work into so go a little further over the edge of the knitting than usual.

Cut and sew can also be used to make alterations. If the garment is too big, take a piece out of the sides or shorten the length. If it is too small, cut it apart, anywhere you like, and insert new sections to make it fit. Any alterations will look like part of the original design if you work with imagination.

OVERLOCKING An overlocking machine will cut and neaten the seam in one go. Make sure you go right to the end of the knitting.

BANDS The width of all the bands, cuffs and other extra bits can be decided on when your garment is almost complete. You can go on making minor adjustments to the finished size. Be prepared to change your ideas at every stage if you find that something is not working or you have a better idea.

FINDING YOUR OWN SOLUTIONS You are certain to encounter problems but there is always a way to get round them. Do not be bound by convention. Use your imagination, use your own ideas. All my methods have come from experimentation. You can do the same.

Applications

Many of the garments described can be seen on the colour pages.

This was knitted in every pastel shade of double knitting that I could find, with white between the squares and for the bands. I made a large ball of yarn (See Complications, page 58.)

The back was to be 56 cm wide with four squares across. That meant each square would have to be 14 cm. I allowed nothing for the white borders to the squares because the amount added by the border is cancelled out by the amount lost picking up stitches. Squares of this size would give a 70 cm long jacket, with sleeves of 42 cm.

I sketched the positions of the squares, similar to the diagram above. When all the whole squares were finished I made full-size drawings of the shaped pieces and knitted to the shapes.

For the white borders I divided the number of stitches on the diagonal by 1.4 and then picked up that number of stitches along each edge. It was all stitched together and white bands added to the bottom, fronts, sleeves and neck. It was fastened with assorted pastel buttons.

Rectangle for back
56 cm x 70 cm

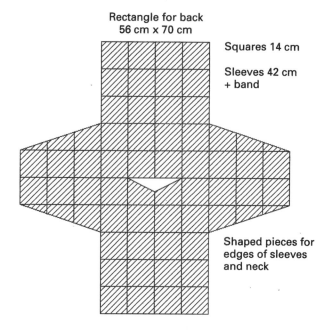

Squares 14 cm

Sleeves 42 cm + band

Shaped pieces for edges of sleeves and neck

Large sleeve bottoms need gathering in with cuffs. Pick up every knobble. Reduce number of stitches on next row. Cast off loosely.

For borders of squares pick up stitches with white double knitting. Cast off loosely on next row.

Compare neck with other bands for stitches.

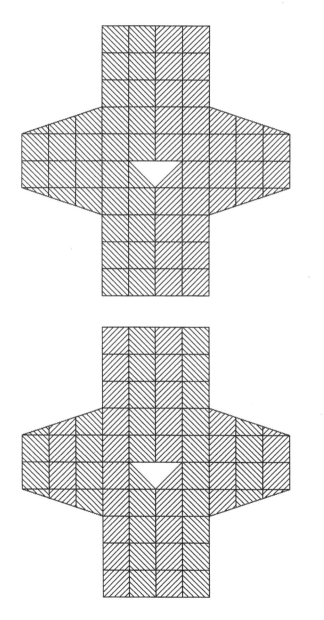

The same squares could be used in different arrangements. The neck shaping would be easier because it could lie along the line of the knitting.

Chevron effects using same basic squares.

Suitable for self-coloured cardigan. Direction of squares would affect shading of design.

The babies' cardigans were made in the same way. Only the colourings and sizes are different.

Babies' and children's clothes are very good for practising on. They don't take as long as adult garments and you can try out ideas on a small scale. However, there seems to be a lot of stitching in proportion to the amount of knitting and, as all the squares are so small, progress can sometimes seem to be very slow.

The finished garment can be as large or small as you want. These were for premature babies, and measured approximately 16" (40 cm) around the chest. Each square was 2" (5 cm). The only shaping is at the neck, where two shapes are only half squares. There are narrow bands all round and the sleeves are pulled in with narrow cuffs.

The green/white and peach/white cardigans (right) show the different effects created by using the same pieces in a different order.

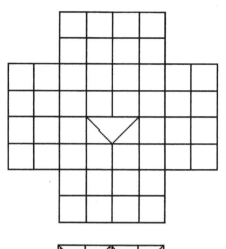

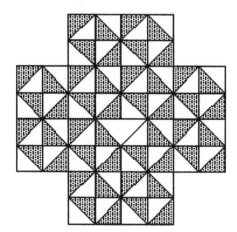

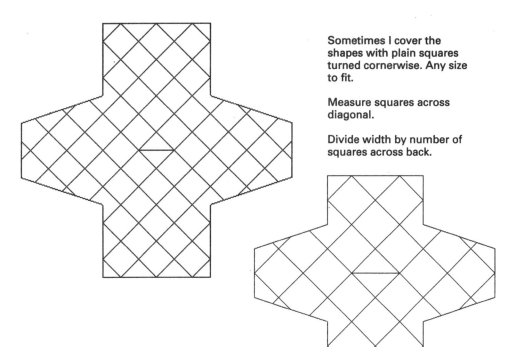

Sometimes I cover the shapes with plain squares turned cornerwise. Any size to fit.

Measure squares across diagonal.

Divide width by number of squares across back.

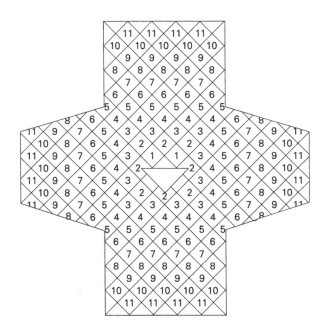

I made this jacket in eleven shades of grey, radiating out from the neck from almost white to black. The numbers indicate the shades. The neckband was in the palest grey, the bottom bands in black and the front bands in sections to match the squares.

Rectangle for back 55 cm x 66 cm.

Two squares of 7, 9 and 11 join front and back.

Sleeves 38.5 cm + deep cuffs.

Squares 11 cm (across diagonal).

Triangles for bottom edge and sleeves. Edges would be pointed without them.

These two designs were made from almost identical squares. The apparent differences come from turning the squares cornerwise in the second version and changing the colours. (See colour pages.) The same pink yarn was used in both although it does not look the same because of the contrasting colours used.

One jacket is slightly wider and shorter than the other and it is pulled in more with a band to give a bloused effect. The sleeves are also wider and pulled in to a tight cuff.

Squares 19 cm diagonally

Top
Rectangle for back 52 x 65 cm.

Sleeve width above cuff 26 cm.

Sleeve length 39 cm + cuff.

Shaped pieces for edges of sleeves.

Cast off along diagonal of two squares for neck.

Bottom
Back 57 cm square.

Sleeve width above cuff 38 cm.

Shaped pieces for edges of sleeves.

Sleeve length 38 cm + cuff.

Some squares and part squares to join front to back.

Triangles at bottom and sleeve bottoms.

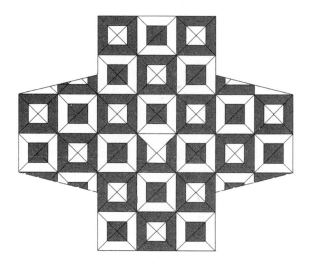

Squares 19 cm diagonally

Some of my designs are made from shapes that are repeated all over the garment, like a wallpaper pattern; some are repeated front and back; others radiate from the neck as the centre. These are only a few of the ways of positioning a design. Invent your own.

The calculations are a bit more complicated but they don't involve much more than careful measuring and dividing up the length and width. If you are uncertain, check your calculations by writing the measurements on every shape and then adding up those that make the width and length.

Remember to check that the design will match at the side seams. If you are not sure, cut out your drawing and fold it into the garment shape. This cube jacket folds to match in all directions.

Back 4 squares wide,
5 squares long

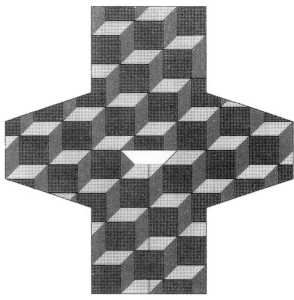

Pick up stitches for parallelograms along edges of squares, knit 7 cm. Cast off.
Number of stitches = diagonal of square divided by 1.4

Rectangle for back
56 x 70 cm.

Sleeves 42 cm + narrow cuff.

Some shapes on side seam wrap round to join back and front.

Shaped pieces for sleeves and neck.

Some part shapes for bottom and bottom of sleeves.

I wanted a jacket in shades of pink and purple. Steve drew this one, with its interesting cubes. The top of one cube may be the bottom of another. The shapes are still very simple, it is the way they fit together that is complex. The colours are very subtle so the complexity of the design is not immediately noticed; I still see something different almost every time I look at it.

I made it from double knitting yarns in eight shades.

The knitting can begin with any of the squares, although working out the size of a starting square is a bit more difficult this time.

Making up the width of the back, there are two straight squares and two diagonal squares. A diagonal is 1.4 times the width of a straight square so the back is 4.8 squares wide. (1 + 1 + 1.4 + 1.4)

Each square has to be the back width divided by 4.8.

The length of the back is 5.8 squares (1 + 1 + 1 + 1.4 + 1.4)

The height of the parallelograms is half the diagonal of the square.

I am very fond of designs that radiate out from the neck. They look nice and can create many different effects. They are also useful for using up yarn because all the sections can be matched at every stage.

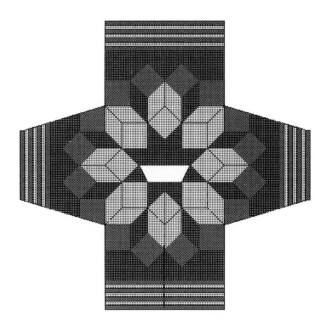

The choice of colours can change the dominant features of any design. When I used the design from the opposite page again I knitted it in thick purple and green mohair yarns. It is very difficult to recognise that it started from the same idea. I combined some of the small shapes to make large hexagons around the neck. The method for knitting this shape can be found in **Complications**, page 60.

This jacket is not completely made from small shapes because I was using up left-over yarns and I was not sure whether there would be enough of each colour. I made the central part, knitted shapes to fit round the edges and then knitted straight across the full width of each piece, working in stripes until the yarns were almost used up. I finished the sleeves before I finished the body because the sleeves had to be the right length to fit properly whereas the length of the body was not so important.

The width of this jacket is the same as the one opposite. The shapes are the same size although the number of stitches needed for each is very different because of the thickness of the yarns.

The length of the patterned area is 2 squares + 1.5 diagonal squares, which makes a total of 4.1 squares.

The design I return to most often is squares in squares in squares. It is worked from the centre squares outwards. I make a centre square, divide the stitches on the diagonal by 1.4, pick up that number of stitches on one edge of the square and knit to a point. When four sides have been done I have a new, larger square. The new square has sides the same length as the diagonal of the first so I pick up the number of stitches I had on the first diagonal. The number of stitches to pick up to complete the next size square is twice the number of the second, and so on.

When the large squares are eventually stitched together the spaces between them make even more squares.

I have used this idea in several versions with varying numbers of squares in squares. I think one of the reasons I find it so interesting is that once I have picked up a row of stitches each row gets shorter until it disappears completely.

I have used squares in squares many times. Cushions are a good way to practise this, and other techniques as well. I made lots of bright pink and black cushions simply because they showed the shapes so effectively. Reversing the colours is particularly noticeable when they are in such sharp contrast.

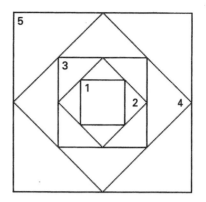

Width of square 2 = diagonal of square 1
Square 3 = twice width of square 1
Square 4 = twice width of square 2
Square 5 = twice width of square 3

Width of centre square
= quarter width of outer square.

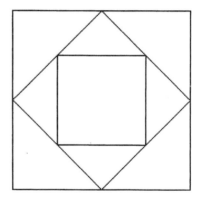

Width of centre square
= half width of outer square.

Divide measurement for back to find size
of starting square.

These jackets are both based on the squares in squares ideas. Each can have several furher variations.

I have made this in double knitting, using two yarns - one plain black, the other a red and black mixture that varied along its length from purple-red to orange-red. Each large square was edged with black before they were stitched together.
  I made it again with a black bouclé and a subtly variegated brushed yarn. The squares were not edged this time, which made the new squares (white on this drawing) particularly interesting.

The first time I made this it was in three shades of thick, fluffy yarn. It looked completely different from the others.
  I have also used two contrasting balls of home-made multi-coloured yarn and this method to make a square large enough for the whole back of a jumper.

N.B. These drawings show no space for the neck. I vary the size of the opening from one garment to another.

The pieces don't have to be small. The jumper doesn't have to be all patchwork. This has patchwork back and front and "normal" sleeves.

The back and front are mirror images of each other, except for the neck shaping. Each is made from a large white triangle with a blue stripe and a large blue triangle with a white stripe. The white triangles were started at the bottom of the jumper, the blue ones at the shoulder. The stripes are immediately below the armhole level and are the same width as the stripes on the sleeves.

For the sleeves I picked up one stitch from each row end between the stripes and knitted down towards the cuff. I worked out how many rows would be needed for the sleeve by counting a similar length on the back. I knew how wide the sleeve should be above the cuff so I could work out how often to decrease to get the right number of stitches.

When sleeves are being worked from the top downwards it is very easy to try on the nearly completed garment to make any final adjustments. This is especially useful for children's clothes, and the sleeves can also be added to later as the children grow.

I knitted the blue and white jumper in three sizes, for Steve and his two sons. The three jumpers were all knitted in exactly the same way. Before I started I knew how big I wanted the finished square to be for each back. I also knew how deep the armholes had to be, and the lengths needed for the sleeves. The width of the stripe was adjusted so it was in roughly the same proportion to each jumper.

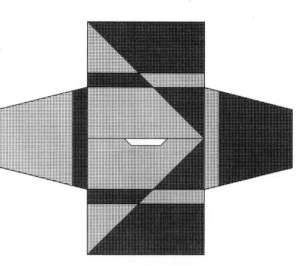

These are the measurements I used:

Steve: Back 56 cm square
          Stripe - 25 cm from
          shoulder, 7 cm wide

Mathew: Back 40 cm square
          Stripe - 17 cm from
          shoulder, 5 cm wide

Richard: Back 32 cm square
          Stripe - 14 cm from
          shoulder, 4 cm wide

94

These are just a few of the garments I have made. I hope there is something here you can use in your own way or to give you new ideas of your own.

Odd lengths of pastel shades of double knitting yarn were used for the squares of this jacket, each square being edged with a white border. See page 84.

Green/white and peach/white cardigans for a very small baby, showing the different effects that can be obtained by arranging the pieces in a different order. The photographs show the shapes sewn together and the finished cardigans. See page 86.

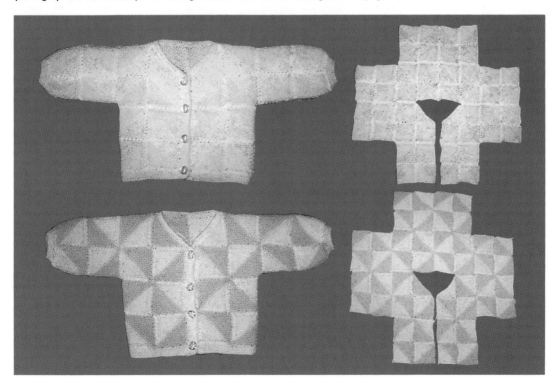

Strikingly patterned jacket in pink and black, the pattern formed by knitting striped squares which can be arranged to give different shapes. See page 88.

Jacket with an all-over pattern of grey, mauve and green cubes, giving a three-dimensional effect. See page 89.

Radiating pattern of cubes in shades of pink and purple for a jacket that looks complicated but is very simple to knit and make up. See page 90.

Squares in squares in squares can create very interesting effects that can be used in many different ways. This sweater in shades of grey uses the pattern to create a bold central design. See page 92.

Cushions are a good way of practising the design. See page 92.

Jacket using black and a mixture of red and black to create an all-over pattern, still using the same basic squares-in-squares design. See page 93.

A simpler use of the same design using three colours. Again, the effect is quite different. See page 93.

You can make a jumper using much larger pieces. This one has two triangles on the front and two on the back. The sleeves are knitted in the conventional way. See page 94.

Calculations

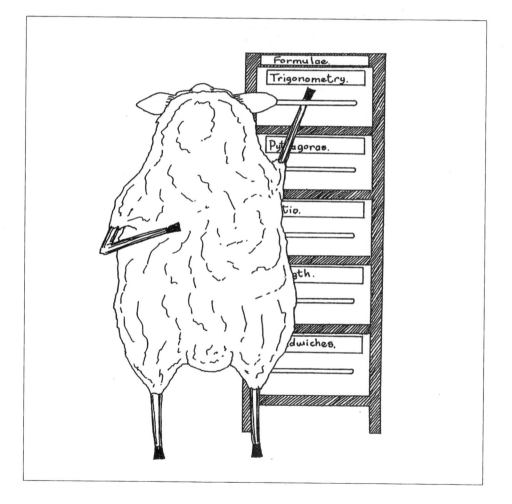

Knitting requires accuracy in counting and measuring, especially when you are creating deliberately geometric shapes. If you count and measure accurately, and take careful note of what you have done so that you can do it again, that's all the maths you really need. You can make all your shapes by drawing and knitting to the drawn shape. You do not have to do elaborate calculations.

On the following pages you will find various charts:

Between the charts you will find explanations of the mathematics, mainly Pythagoras' Theorem and trigonometry, which leads to the entries in some of the charts. You do not need to read these explanations to be able to use the charts but you may find the mathematics of interest.

It is extremely difficult to assess the amount of yarn accurately. It does not help if you try to compare with stocking stitch patterns because the proportions of the stitches are not the same. Garter stitch has fewer stitches but more rows. Garter stitch comes out a little thicker than stocking stitch and overall more yarn is needed. The thicker the yarn you choose, the more you will need, and the more expensive your garment is likely to be.

The chart shows approximate amounts of yarn needed for a fairly close-fitting average length jumper. If possible allow more yarn than this, although you will sometimes find you need considerably less. (The three blue and white jumpers in **Applications** were made out of a total of less than 800 grams.)

Yarn	Child age 6 - 8	Average woman	Average man
4 ply	250 - 350 grams	350 -450 grams	450 - 550 grams
Double knitting	300 - 400 grams	400 - 500 grams	500 - 600 grams
Aran	400 - 500 grams	500 - 600 grams	600 - 700 grams
Chunky	450 - 550 grams	550 - 700 grams	700 - 900 grams

If you want to try to work out how much yarn you need from the pieces you have already made you may find it easier to work with area than with weight. You might be able to weigh some pieces on the kitchen scales so you can estimate the total weight of yarn you need. Otherwise knit one complete ball and see how many pieces it will give you. Estimate how many more of those pieces you will need and thereby discover how many balls you need.

If you are working in several colours this can be quite complicated, and there is no easy way to do it: every design will be different in the proportions of the yarns it uses. You can only do it by comparing pieces you have made, and even then the results will be altered by using different yarns. It will have to be mainly guesswork, with some logical mathematics to give an approximate amount. Always buy more yarn than you think you need. It is better to have too much than not enough.

GUIDE TO SIZES

Use these guides to help you design your own garments. Your measurements might be very different from these and still be right. Double check if you are in any doubt.

GUIDE TO MEASUREMENTS FOR MEN – IN INCHES

Finished chest measurement	38	40	42	44	46	48
Length from back neck	25	25.5	26	26.5	27	27.5
Sleeve seam	18.5	18.5	19	19	19.5	19.5
Armhole depth	9.5	9.5	10	10	10.5	10.5
Wrist above cuff	9	9	9.5	9.5	10	10
Width of back neck	7	7	7.5	7.5	8	8
Depth of round neck	3	3	3	3.5	3.5	3.5

GUIDE TO MEASUREMENTS FOR WOMEN – IN INCHES

Finished bust measurement	34	36	38	40	42	44
Length – sweater	21	21.5	22	22.5	23	23.5
Length – long cardigan	25	25.5	26	26.5	27	27.5
Sleeve seam	17	17	17.5	17.5	18	18
Armhole depth	8	8.5	9	9.5	10	10
Wrist above cuff	7.5	8	8.5	9	9.5	10
Width of back neck	6	6	6.5	6.5	7	7
Depth of round neck	3	3	3	3	3	3

GUIDE TO MEASUREMENTS FOR CHILDREN – IN INCHES

Age	2	3-4	5-6	7-8	9-10	11-12
Height	36	40	44	48	52	56
Finished chest measurement	22	24	26	28	30	32
Length	13	14	15.	17	19	21
Sleeve seam	9	10	11	13	14	15
Armhole depth	5	5.5	6	6.5	7	7.5
Wrist above cuff	5	5.5	6	6.5	7	7.5
Width of back neck	4.5	5	5	5.5	5.5	6
Depth of round neck	2	2.5	2.5	3	3	3

Remember that the chest and wrist measurements are
all the way round, not just the back. Work in
centimetres or inches, whichever you find easier.

GUIDE TO MEASUREMENTS FOR MEN – IN CENTIMETRES

Finished chest measurement	97	102	107	112	117	122
Length from back neck	63.5	65	66	67	68.5	70
Sleeve seam	47	47.5	48	48.5	49	49.5
Armhole depth	24	24.5	25	26	26.5	27
Wrist above cuff	23	23.5	24	24.5	25	25.5
Width of back neck	18	18.5	19	19.5	20	20.5
Depth of round neck	7.5	7.5	8	8	8.5	8.5

GUIDE TO MEASUREMENTS FOR WOMEN – IN CENTIMETRES

Finished bust measurement	87	92	97	102	107	112
Length – sweater	53	54.5	56	57	58.5	60
Length – long cardigan	63.5	65	66	67	68.5	70
Sleeve seam	43	43.5	44.5	45	45.5	46
Armhole depth	20	21.5	23	24	25	26
Wrist above cuff	19	20	21.5	23	24	25.5
Width of back neck	15	16	16.5	17	17.5	18
Depth of round neck	7.5	7.5	7.5	7.5	7.5	7.5

GUIDE TO MEASUREMENTS FOR CHILDREN – IN CENTIMETRES

Age	2	3-4	5-6	7-8	9-10	11-12
Height	92	102	112	122	132	142
Finished chest measurement	56	61	66	71	76	81
Length	33	35.5	38	43	48	53
Sleeve seam	23	25.5	28	33	35.5	38
Armhole depth	12.5	14	15	16.5	18	19
Wrist above cuff	12.5	14	15	16.5	18	19
Width of back neck	11.5	12	12.5	13.5	14	15
Depth of round neck	5	6	6.5	7	7.5	7.5

All calculations should be based on a square somewhere in your design. The size of that square should be carefully worked out from the width of the garment. (See the examples in **Applications**.) On the opposite page are squares from 6 cm to 14 cm. Whole numbers are easier to calculate but you may have to work with more precise sizes.

All shapes will have to be knitted very accurately to ensure that they fit together. It is easier to measure the knitting against a cut-out shape than on the page where there are several confusing outlines. Cut out the size you want, preferably from card. Cut out any other shapes you intend to make, once you have calculated their sizes and angles. You could cut out every shape to make sure they will all fit together to give the correct garment size, but all that is really needed is one template for each shape.

An error of half a centimetre per shape will be magnified to eight times that if you have four squares across the back and four across the front. That would make a difference of four centimetres around your garment. The more shapes you have, the bigger the error will become. You can round up or down a little to suit your own purposes if you are aware what effect that will have overall. You might overcome problems by rounding up for one shape and down for the next. (Shapes that are meant to match must be identical or it might be noticeable.) These individual alterations are so tiny they should not make any significant difference.

A calculator is vital for your calculations. The answers it gives may be confusing. The display may give you six, or more, decimal places and you will never need more than one. Look at the first two numbers after the decimal point and forget all the rest. If the second of those numbers is 5, 6, 7, 8 or 9 you should round up the first decimal place to the next number. Any other number should be ignored.

In practice you will not be able to work to nearer than one decimal place, and perhaps not even that if your yarn is thick. It is easier to be accurate with thin yarns as the stitches are so small they allow more variety of measurements to be achieved. Be as accurate as is practically possible. You will probably have to work to the nearest half centimetre.

If you are working in inches instead of centimetres, remember that 0.5 is half an inch, 0.25 is a quarter of an inch and 0.75 is three quarters of an inch. You will

EXAMPLE

5.4**6**735 rounds to 5.5
5.4**4**735 rounds to 5.4

probably want to work to the nearest quarter inch.

Accuracy, at all stages, is the key to getting the garment you want. It is easy to get it right if you measure everything carefully. Do not guess. Do not be content with a piece that is nearly right, it has to be as close as you can make it. Do not stretch shapes to make them the right size.

All knitwear design is based on precise mathematical procedures. It may begin with a creative idea but could never take shape without the maths.

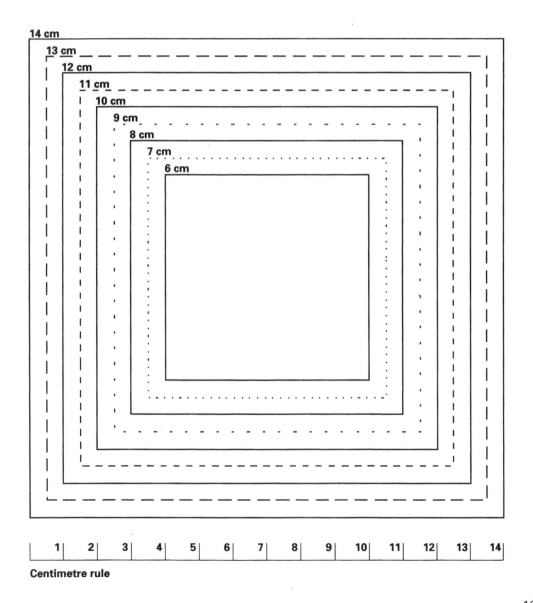

Centimetre rule

In a right-angled triangle, the square of the length of the hypotenuse is equal to the sum of the squares of the lengths of the other two sides.

This theorem was named after Pythagoras of Samos, a Greek philosopher who led a group of religious and scientific thinkers, over two thousand years ago. It has been proved many times since, using a large variety of methods. If you would like to know how to prove it, the maths section of your library should provide plenty of information. One published book contains 367 proofs. For most people, knowing how to use the theorem is more important than why it works.

Hypotenuse (long side) = 5
Other sides = 3 and 4
Theorem:

$$5^2 = 3^2 + 4^2$$

$$(5 \times 5) = (3 \times 3) + (4 \times 4)$$

$$25 = 9 + 16$$

When you were working out how many stitches to pick up along the edge of a square you were using Pythagoras' theorem.

A square is made up of two right-angled triangles. You need to concentrate on one of them to work out your measurements. This triangle is a special use of Pythagoras because it has both of 'the other sides' the same length.

Imagine each of the shorter sides to be one unit long.
The square of the hypotenuse $= 1^2 + 1^2$

$$= (1 \times 1) + (1 \times 1)$$
$$= 1 + 1$$
$$= 2$$

Hypotenuse = the square root of 2.
The calculator gives this as 1.4142136.

It is an irrational number. It disappears off the end of the calculator display but cannot be perfectly worked out however many decimal places you work to. For your calculations you can work with 1.4.

The ratio between the side of a square and its diagonal is always 1 : 1.4

You can use the ratio of 1 : 1.4 with measurements or with numbers of stitches.

If you know the length of the diagonal of a square , in stitches, centimetres or inches, divide it by 1.4 to find the length of the side. The answer will be just over two thirds of the diagonal.

If you know the length of the side, multiply by 1.4 to find the diagonal. The diagonal will always be almost one and a half times the length of the side of the square.

When you are working with measurements decide on your own degree of accuracy. When you are working with numbers of stitches you will have to round to a whole number. You cannot pick up half a stitch.

The chart below gives some of the sizes you may be using. It has no units because it works for centimetres, inches or stitches.

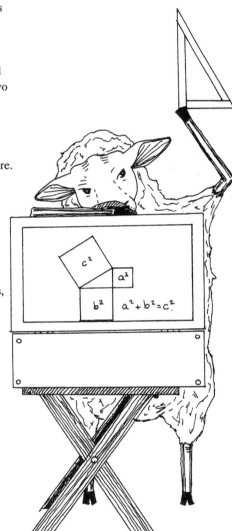

Diagonal	5	6	7	8	9	10	11	12	13	14	15	16
Side	3.5	4.2	5.0	5.7	6.4	7.1	7.8	8.5	9.2	9.9	10.6	11.3
Diagonal	17	18	19	20	21	22	23	24	25	26	27	28
Side	12.0	12.7	13.4	14.1	14.9	15.6	16.3	17.0	17.7	18.4	19.1	19.8
Diagonal	29	30	31	32	33	34	35	36	37	38	39	40
Side	20.5	21.2	21.9	22.6	23.3	24.0	24.8	25.5	26.2	26.9	27.6	28.3

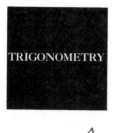

TRIGONOMETRY

Trigonometry is a branch of mathematics that deals with the relationships between the sides and angles of triangles. It is based on the fact that triangles with the same size angles have their sides in the same ratio to each other.

These are two similar triangles. Mathematically that means their angles are the same and corresponding sides are in the same proportion.

In this example each side of the small triangle is half the length of the corresponding side in the large triangle.

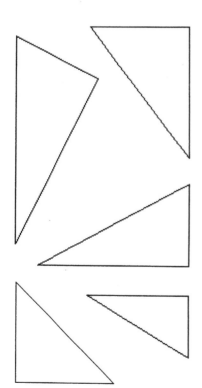

Trigonometry is most often used with right-angled triangles when the sides are named and used in three different combinations to work out ratios.

As in all right-angled triangles, the side facing the right angle is called the **hypotenuse.** The other two sides are named in relation to the angle you want to work with. The side facing the angle you are using for your calculations is known as the **opposite** side. The side next to that angle is called the **adjacent** side. They are shortened to hyp, opp and adj.

The three ratios are known as **sine, cosine** and **tangent** and these are usually abbreviated to sin, cos and tan. The rules to use are:

1. To find the cosine: divide the length of the adjacent side by the length of the hypotenuse.
2. To find the sine: divide the length of the opposite side by the length of the hypotenuse.
3. To find the tangent: divide the length of the opposite side by the length of the adjacent.

Use the inverse functions of a scientific calculator to find the size of the angle you have. The tan, cos and sin buttons tell you the ratios of the sides when you already know the angles. Inverse tan, inverse cos and inverse sin tell you the angles when you know the ratios.

You can also use the trigonometry rules to find the length of a side if you already know the sizes of one of the angles and one of the sides. Write down the formula you need, put in any information you know and then work out the unknown.

Increasing at only one side of the work will create a right-angled triangle; increasing at both sides will not. The diagrams below show the different effects. The shapes that are increased at both sides can be treated as two right-angled triangles joined together. Each small rectangle represents one stitch. Remember that a garter stitch ridge is made up of two rows.

For the increasings to be evenly spaced you will sometimes have to work them at the end of the row and sometimes at the start, depending on which side of the work you need them to be. The four diagrams below show the different combinations you could be using.

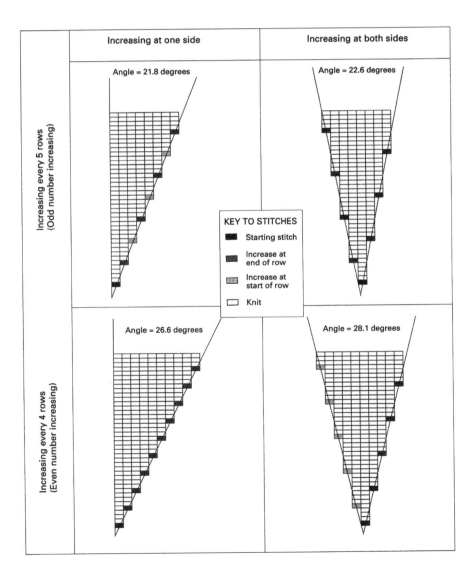

USING

TRIGONOMETRY

The rules of trigonometry can be used to calculate the angles or lengths for any of the shaped pieces you might decide to knit. They are simple to use for garter stitch shapes because one ridge (two rows) is the same height as the width of one stitch. They will work with other stitches but other factors then have to be taken into consideration.

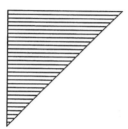

INCREASING ONE EDGE, ALTERNATE
ROWS Increase at the right-hand side on alternate rows so that you are increasing one stitch on each ridge. The number of ridges is the same as the number of stitches.

tan x (bottom angle) = opp (number of stitches) divided by adj (number of ridges). In this triangle those numbers are the same so the division will always have the answer 1. The angle with a tangent of 1 is 45 degrees.

INCREASING ONE EDGE, EVERY FOURTH
ROW Increase every fourth row at the right and there will always be twice as many ridges as stitches.

tan x = opp(stitches) divided by adj (rows).
In this triangle the ridges are always twice the number of stitches so the answer is always 0.5.
The angle is 26.6 degrees.

INCREASING
ALTERNATE EDGES,
EVERY FOURTH ROW
(= increasing both edges, every second row). This can be knitted in one piece but the angle is worked out as the total from two right-angled triangles joined together.
Each triangle is increased every fourth row (every second ridge). In each triangle the tan ratio gives an angle of 26.56 degrees so the combined angle is 53,1 degrees

INCREASING DIFFERENTLY
ON EACH EDGE

The triangles do not have to be alike. The
one on the left increases every second ridge
so the tan ratio gives an angle of 26.56
degrees. The triangle on the right increases
every third ridge so the tan ratio is 0.33, which
gives an angle of 18.4 degrees. The total is almost
45 degrees.

The table overleaf shows what size angle you get if you
increase with regular frequency. Both columns give the
angle you will get if you increase one stitch on the rows
shown. This always works because of the relationship
between the number of ridges and the number of
stitches. It has nothing to do with the thickness of your
yarn or your tension.

The new stitches create a series of little steps along
the side of the work but once the pieces are joined
together that looks like a straight line. Knitting can
always be stretched a little so, in most cases, you should
choose the most appropriate angle from the table. For
some angles you will need to experiment and alternate
the frequency of increases.

Decreasing, instead of increasing will create exactly
the same angles except they will be areas taken off the
knitting, not added to it.

Frequency of increase	Angle produced by increasing at both edges (degrees)	Angle produced by increasing at one edge (degrees)
Every row	90.0	63.4
Every 2nd row	53.1	45.0
Every 3rd row	36.9	33.7
Every 4th row	28.1	26.6
Every 5th row	22.6	21.8
Every 6th row	18.9	18.4
Every 7th row	16.3	15.9
Every 8th row	14.3	14.0
Every 9th row	12.7	12.5
Every 10th row	11.4	11.3
Every 11th row	10.4	10.3
Every 12th row	9.5	9.5
Every 13th row	8.8	8.8
Every 14th row	8.2	8.1
Every 15th row	7.6	7.6
Every 16th row	7.2	7.1
Every 17th row	6.7	6.7
Every 18th row	6.4	6.3
Every 19th row	6.0	6.0
Every 20th row	5.7	5.7

Explorations

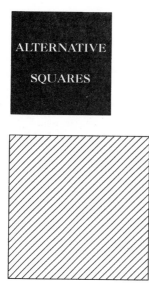

The method of making a square that you have used so far is probably the easiest for a beginner to use. It is not the only way and you might now want to experiment to see if you would prefer another way.

Using the same basic method there are many different ways of increasing and decreasing at the beginnings or ends of rows. If you know other methods, try them. If you don't you can look in other knitting books.

Some methods will leave loops, which make it very easy to pick up stitches but could give a slightly lacy effect. Some give more pronounced ridges, which you might want to incorporate into your design. Some make the edges of the work very tight and so difficult to pick up stitches. Try as many methods as you can find for both increasing and decreasing. Use whichever you find most satisfactory. You might discover that some are more suitable for use with some yarns than with others.
Explore!

The actual knitting of the squares can be very tedious, especially on the short rows at the beginning of each square. Some people find it very irritating to be constantly turning the work. I overcome this by using very short needles, intended for children, to start each square, and if the square is small enough I work it all on these needles. Other people solve the problem by doing backwards knitting. They do not turn the work round, they just work back along the row from the opposite end, reversing all the processes.

All knitting is a matter of habit. The method you are used to is always the one you find easiest, but do bear in mind that there are many other ways of doing it.
Explore!

Another fairly accurate way of making a square that will come out to the right size without having to work out the tension first is to knit on four needles, from the centre of the square outwards. When making squares five needles are much better, however, because you can have the stitches for each side on one needle and you can easily lay the work down flat to measure it.

Start with eight stitches joined into a ring and put two on each needle. Increase at both ends of each needle on alternate rows. Working on needles like this gives the same effect as working on circular needles. If

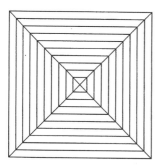

you go round and round doing only knit stitches you will get stocking stitch, not garter stitch. If you want it to look like garter stitch, work backwards and forwards and stitch up the gap that you are left with. You could also try knitting and purling alternately although this is not completely satisfactory where the rounds join.

I do not like this method. It is very fiddly at the centre and difficult to work in garter stitch, although it is more satisfactory in other stitches. It does not give the same degree of accuracy as the first way because you have to add one row at each side on every round. In thick yarns this can make a significant difference.

The commonest way of knitting a square is to cast on several stitches, knit until the work is square and cast off again. It is possible to get a perfect square this way but it is extremely difficult to get a perfect square of the exact size you need. It will work if you always knit with the same size needles, using exactly the same thickness of yarn and work to the same tension. Another person using the same yarn and needles would probably get a different size square because the tension would not be the same. Knitters do not work exactly alike, which is why commercial patterns always insist you work a tension square before you start. It is a very necessary precaution when you are following a pattern, but not needed for these patchwork shapes.

Apart from the difficulties of getting the size right, it is also quite a problem to keep the edges of the shape square. There are several methods of casting on and casting off and some of them are better than others. Many people have problems with one, or both, edges curling up and distorting the shape.

Oxfam publish a leaflet which gives the number of stitches considered to be the right amount to make six-inch squares for blankets, in varying thicknesses of yarn. It is probably quite satisfactory for blankets but would not give the required degree of accuracy for garments. You could use it as a guide, but if you really want to knit squares in this way you ought to make a sample for each different yarn you are going to use and work out how many stitches and rows are needed. Keep a record of your results and you won't need to make another sample next time you use the same yarn.

These squares can be put together in a variety of ways and you could even mix the different methods of making squares in any way you want.

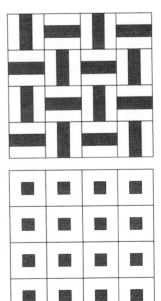

113

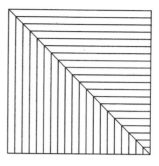

MAGIC SQUARES

Starting at the outside edge:
Cast on an even number of stitches and put a loop of a different coloured yarn round the needle between the middle two stitches.
Row 1 Knit until you reach two stitches before the marker, knit two together, move the marker onto the other needle, knit two together, knit to the end of the row.
Row 2 Knit.
Repeat these two rows. On alternate rows you will be decreasing two stitches at the centre of the row, one each side of the marker. Continue until two stitches remain. Knit together and fasten off.
As you have been knitting the work will have folded inwards and magically turned into a square with the cast-on edge forming two of the sides and row ends forming the others.

Starting at the centre: Cast on two stitches.
Row 1 Increase in the first stitch, put a loop on the needle to act as a marker, increase in the other stitch.
Row 2 Knit.
Row 3 Knit to the stitch before the marker, increase in the next stitch, move the marker to the other needle, increase in the next stitch, knit to the end.
Repeat the last two rows until the square is the size you want.
Cast off.

This is known as a magic square because it starts as a straight row of knitting and magically turns into a square.

It can be knitted in two different ways, either from the outside inwards or from the centre outwards (which does not seem so magical).

The two methods produce squares which look almost identical. The first way is fun to do because of the way it turns into a square, but you need to know how many stitches to cast on at the start to get the size square you want. Remember that the cast-on row makes two sides of the square, not one.

The second method is much better for accurate sizing. At the end of every row you have a square so you can keep knitting until the square is the right size, then cast off.

The overall effect of both of these methods is the same as making two of the 45° triangles you have made before, but they are already joined together. You could make the triangles separately and join them, but making them ready joined will probably give you more ideas for new designs.

There is a lot of scope for making designs with these shapes. They can be striped and joined in many ways. Take extra care with the joining. Lines that should be straight look messy if they don't quite meet.

These squares still do not have the versatility of the original ones because they cannot easily be adapted to make other shapes. **Explore!**

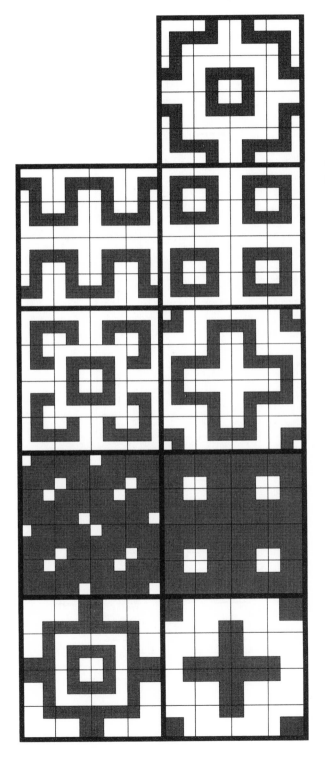

These patterns are
made from 16 of these

These two patterns are
made from 16 of these

These two patterns are made
from a mixture of these

UNEQUAL
SQUARES

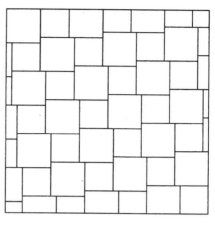

Any two squares can be used together to make a repeating pattern.

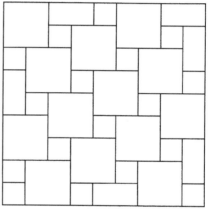

Three different squares can be combined to make a repeating pattern. In this example the width of the two smaller squares added together is the same as the width of the largest square.

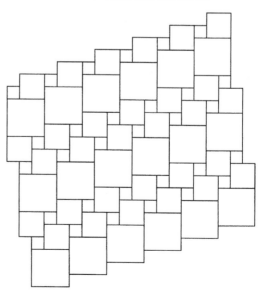

For many years mathematicians tried to divide a square into unequal squares. In 1939 Roland Sprague did it using 55 different squares. In 1978 A.J.W. Duijvestijn found the solution shown here. It uses 21 different squares.

If you halve the measurements given and use them as the sides of your squares, in centimetres, you will get a square of 56cm.

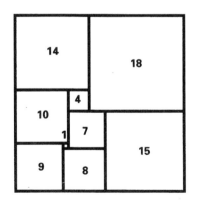

This smaller drawing is not a square. It is a rectangle with dimensions of 32 by 33 units. It is divided into 9 different squares. The difference between the width and the length is so little that it could be used as the front or back of a jumper and no one would be likely to notice that it is not a square. The numbers given could not be used as the dimensions of the squares, unless you want the jumper to be child size. If they are taken as the diagonals of the squares, in inches, you would get a square of approximately 23".

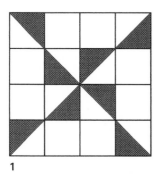

WHAT IS A PATTERN?

How do you differentiate between a pattern and an abstract design? What makes a pattern?

Most people would define designs that have some sort of symmetry as patterns, perhaps without ever knowing why they would choose some and not others.

Regular patterns are formed by three basic processes used in different combinations:
1. Moving the shape to a new positiion without altering it in any other way.
2. Turning the shape round when it is moved.
3. Flipping the shape over when it is moved.

There are two types of symmetry which you might be able to find in any design you recognise as a pattern. They are rotation and reflection symmetry. If a pattern has rotation symmetry it means that it will fit onto itself in another position when you turn it round. A pattern has reflection symmetry if you could put a mirror across the design so that what you see in the mirror is what you see in real life. A design can have both types of symmetry at the same time.

Repeating patterns are very precisely defined in some maths books. According to those definitions there are 7 possible strip patterns (which are shown opposite with the ways of deriving them) and another 17 wallpaper patterns. You could use any of these or a pattern which does not fit into these categories.

If you repeat shapes but change the colours, are you repeating the pattern? Mathematically you are, but you might consider that the mathematical rules do not apply in such circumstances.

If you repeat shapes when the whole design is the same colour, have you made a pattern at all?

People's ideas of what constitutes a pattern vary a great deal. Do whatever you want to do. You can call it whatever you like. Whether it makes a pattern or not is irrelevant, but do take care not to end up with a random pattern that looks as though it's been thrown together with no thought.

Explore patterns.

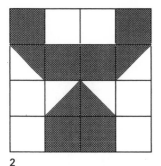

1

1 This will fit onto itself in four different positions. It is said to have rotation symmetry of order 4. It has no lines of reflection.

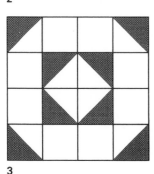

2

2 This has one line of reflection, down the middle. It has no rotation symmetry.

3

3 This has rotation symmetry of order 4 and 4 lines of reflection, which are from top to bottom, side to side and both diagonals.

THE SEVEN STRIP PATTERNS

The original square is repeated all along the line.

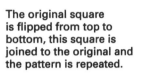

The original square is flipped from top to bottom, this square is joined to the original and the pattern is repeated.

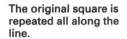

The original is turned half-way round, the two are joined, and the pattern repeated.

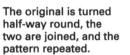

The original is flipped from left to right, the two squares joined, and the pattern repeated.

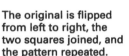

The original square is followed by a sideways flip, a top-to-bottom flip and a half-turned square.

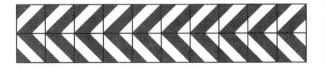

The original is again flipped from top to bottom, the two are joined by a different edge, and the pattern repeated.

The original is joined to a top to bottom flipped square, a side-to-side flipped square and a half-turned square.

119

Optical illusions can be created almost as easily as in drawing. The effects rely on the careful choice of colour. Dark colours usually appear to be nearer and light ones are in the distance.

Some of the garments in **Applications** are optical illusions. The simplest is probably the repeating pattern of cubes. The simple designs are often most effective as others become confused as they wrap round the body.

Illusions can be created with repeat patterns or a single design. Use these at any size you like, either as a single motif, or repeated.

These are a few simple examples, all of which start with a square. Traditional fabric patchwork sometimes uses illusions with squares. **Explore** and invent your own.

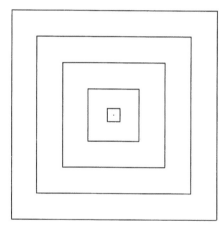

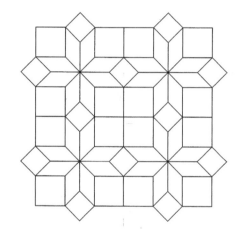

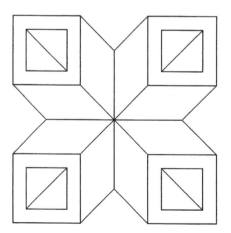

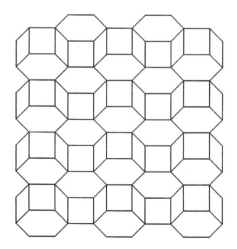

Some shapes can be interlocked to give interesting effects. The first design consists entirely of similar pieces made up of a triangle and a square joined to make an arrow. Alternate rows point in opposite directions and the effect can be very variable, according to the choice of colours. Try copying this design several times and colouring it in various combinations, some sharply contrasting and others only slightly differing. You could limit yourself to two shades, or try more. The second design is a more complicated version of the arrows.

Many shapes can be made to interlock. **Explore** the woodcuts of the Dutch artist M.C.Escher for sources of inspiration.

INTERLOCKING

SHAPES

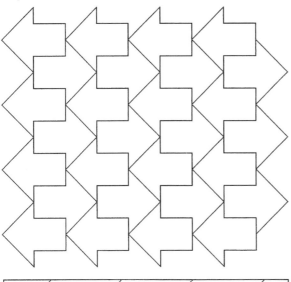

EVER – DECREASING SPIRALS

A spiral is 'a curve formed by a point winding round a fixed point at an ever-increasing distance from it' so these shapes should not really be called spirals.

If you decide to knit them, think carefully about the background pieces needed to fill in the gaps. Some of them are more complicated than the parts of the spiral.

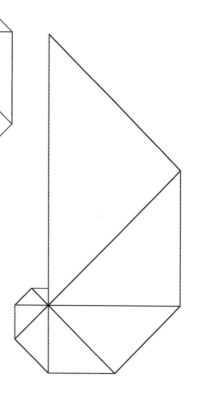

Explore other shapes that could be fitted together to spiral across your jumper or all the way round your body.

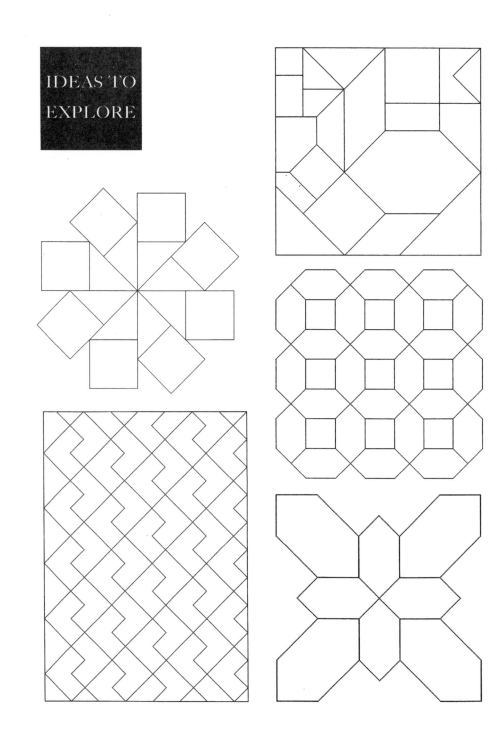

IDEAS TO EXPLORE

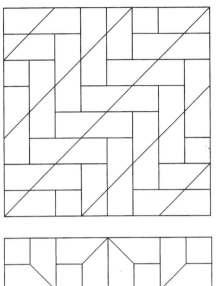

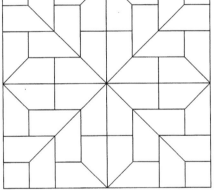
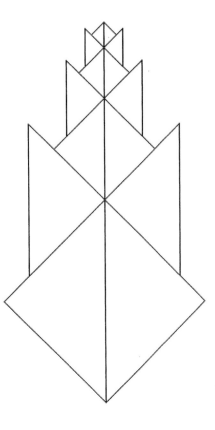
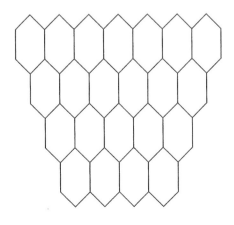

There is no end to the combinations of simple shapes you could use. Colours give even more variety. When you get bored you could move on to using more complex shapes in similar ways. By now you must have plenty of ideas of your own.

Do not follow like a sheep.

USE YOUR IMAGINATION.

EXPLORE.

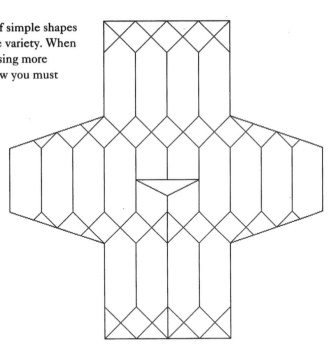

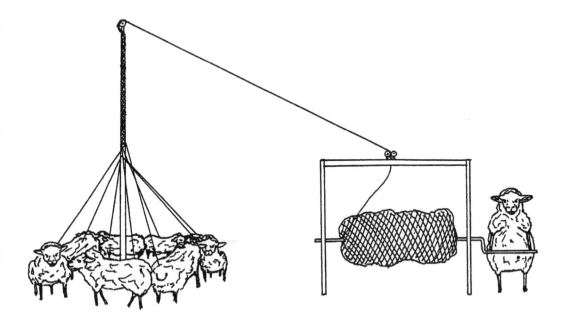